ALASKA'S
Seashore
CREATURES
A Guide to Selected Marine Invertebrates

CARMEN M. FIELD • CONRAD J. FIELD

ALASKA NORTHWEST BOOKS™
Anchorage • Seattle • Portland

To the young explorers in our family, Ian and Taylor

ACKNOWLEDGMENTS • Many people have helped us in the creation of this book by giving phone and personal interviews, sending publications, providing logistical support for our research and photographic forays, and most importantly inspiring us to study marine life through their writings and teachings. We extend special thanks to Roger and Kathy Herrnsteen for their gift of a computer, and for their time assisting us with photographic efforts; Eugene Kozloff for his review of our nomenclature and for the impact his writings have had on our appreciation of marine invertebrates; Stan Eller for his willingness to review the manuscript despite his numerous other commitments; Jack Montgomery and Fran Quinlan for boat transportation, as well as for their enthusiasm for marine education; Karen Willows for training us on our new camera and suggesting how to improve our images; Karin Emig and Bob Halpin for their constant support, use of their computer, and boat transportation; the Pratt Museum for allowing us to "borrow" aquarium invertebrates; and the editorial staff at Alaska Northwest Books, especially Don Graydon, Deborah Loop, and Ellen Wheat, for their patience and direction.

Text and photos copyright © 1999 by Carmen M. Field and Conrad J. Field

Illustrations copyright © 1999 by Conrad J. Field

Library of Congress Cataloging-in-Publication Data
Field, Carmen, 1963–
    Alaska's seashore creatures : a guide to selected marine invertebrates / by Carmen & Conrad Field.
        p.   cm. — (An Alaskan pocket guide)
    Includes bibliographical references and index.
    ISBN 0-88240-516-0
    1. Marine invertebrates—Alaska.   I. Field, Conrad, 1961– . II. Title.
III. Series: Alaska pocket guide
QL365.4.U6F54   1999
592.177'434—dc21   98-30918
                                                            CIP

President/Publisher: Charles M. Hopkins; Editorial Staff: Douglas A. Pfeiffer, Ellen Harkins Wheat, Timothy W. Frew, Alicia I. Paulson, Deborah J. Loop, Joanna M. Goebel; Production Staff: Richard L. Owsiany, Susan Dupere

Editor: Don Graydon; Designer: Michelle Taverniti; Map: Gray Mouse Graphics

PHOTOS: Front cover: blood star; Back cover: opalescent nudibranch; Pages 1–2, 95–96: blue mussels; 3: green sea urchin; 5: lion's mane jellyfish

Alaska Northwest Books™
An imprint of Graphic Arts Center Publishing Company
P.O. Box 10306, Portland, OR 97296-0306 / 503-226-2402

Printed on acid- and elemental-chlorine-free recycled paper in the United States of America

Contents

Alaska's Seashore Creatures

The shores of Alaska support a wealth of fascinating marine creatures. While fishing, beachcombing, or tide-pooling, you'll encounter the stars of this book: the marine invertebrates, ocean animals without backbones. You can find clams, snails, sea stars, barnacles, crabs, marine worms, and many other marine invertebrates simply by exploring the shoreline at low tide.

Some of these spineless wonders live at or above the high-tide line, but as you walk toward the water on receding tides, the beach comes alive with an array of animals unparalleled on dry land. Other marine invertebrates don't appear at the water's edge, preferring to live on the ocean floor in deep water or in the open sea drifting with the currents.

As you look through this pocket guide, you'll learn to identify many of Alaska's common seashore creatures and discover how these intriguing animals make a living: where they are found, how large they grow, what they like to eat, and how they avoid predators. The animals included in the book were chosen because they are often seen (or eaten) in Alaska or because they best represent a group of closely related invertebrates of the Alaskan coast. True sea stars and Sitka periwinkles are invertebrates you'll see often on Alaska's beaches. Pacific razor clams and Bairdi tanner crabs are among the animals people love to eat.

We also included animals that might elude us but are fascinating nonetheless: gumboot chitons, for their enormous size; opalescent nudibranchs, for their bright coloration; cone worms, for their unique home construction. While this small volume can't be a comprehensive guide to Alaska's marine invertebrates, it does feature a broadly diverse group of animals encountered by visitors to the shore.

We share our own observations, as well as the findings of others, in the pages of this guide. Most of the featured species have not been extensively studied. Anyone exploring the coastline, regardless of scientific training or experience, has an opportunity to discover something new and wonderful about Alaska's marine life.

A variety of marine creatures may be discovered beneath intertidal rocks.

ALASKA'S COAST: A SPECIAL PLACE FOR SEASHORE CREATURES

• A myriad of invertebrates have adapted to life in Alaska's cold and stormy seas in order to take advantage of food-rich coastal water. They are especially active during the summer, when microscopic floating plants—the phytoplankton—grow abundantly, thanks to the long, light-filled Alaskan days. The plants are food for small marine animals, which in turn are eaten by larger organisms, and so on up the food chain.

Many marine invertebrates colonize such places as the open ocean, the seafloor, and forests of floating kelp. But the environment that supports the greatest diversity of these animals (and the place most accessible to us) is the intertidal zone—that part of the shoreline that lies between the highest and lowest reaches of the tide.

The intertidal zone has many faces. It includes sandy and muddy flats, as well as eelgrass beds and salt marshes. Or it can be rocky with boulders or gravel or bedrock. Intertidal animals endure a wide range of conditions as they become exposed to the air twice each day with the outgoing tide. They must withstand the drying effects of sun and wind, rapid changes in temperature, possible flooding by freshwater, and heavy wave action. Predators from the sea threaten them at high tide, while land predators move in when the tide is low.

You can think of the coastline as being made up of a series of strips that run parallel to the shore, each with its own tidal influences and community of animals. Farthest from the water is the first of these strips, the splash zone. Organisms that live here, including some acorn barnacles, are beyond the reach of most high tides, feeding only when submerged by an occasional extreme high tide or splashed by waves.

Next comes the intertidal zone, further divided into three strips: the high, middle, and low intertidal zones. The high intertidal zone is covered by water only when the tide is at or near its highest reach. This area provides a habitat suitable for marine animals like beach hoppers and periwinkles. They thrive here because they can withstand long periods of exposure to air each day—and many of their predators can't.

Animals in the middle intertidal zone first become exposed to the air about 2½ hours after high tide. On rocky shores, blue mussel beds and the brown algae commonly called rockweed characterize this middle area. The upper edge of the mussel beds and rockweed defines the boundary between high and middle intertidal zones, and their lower edge is the border between middle and lower.

The lower intertidal zone extends to the water's edge at extreme low tide. This area is often covered in lush growths of red and brown algae and has the greatest diversity of marine creatures. Organisms that live here start to become exposed about an hour and a half before low tide.

Below the intertidal zone is the subtidal zone. The very edge of this deepwater habitat is occasionally exposed during extreme low, or minus, tides. Some nearshore invertebrates, such as sunflower sea stars, are sensitive to being exposed to the air and can retreat with the tide into this realm. Other animals, such as sea peaches and sand dollars, may live permanently within the subtidal zone.

You can explore the margin of the subtidal zone by visiting a beach during one of the year's minus tides. You can also enter this zone by diving, especially during the winter when a seasonal lack of microscopic plants and animals makes for better visibility.

THE LIFE OF A MARINE INVERTEBRATE •
Alaska's marine invertebrates represent many different lifestyles. Microscopic animals known as zooplankton, for example, drift in the ocean at the mercy of wind and currents. Other invertebrates lead a bottom-dwelling life of crawling or burrowing. Still others remain fixed in one place for most of their life.

Marine invertebrates may be herbivorous (eating only plants, such as algae), carnivorous (eating only animals, such as other invertebrates or fish), or omnivorous (eating both plants and animals). Limpets are herbivores, moon snails are carnivores, and brittle stars have it both ways.

Some invertebrates, such as butter clams and sponges, are filter-feeders. They get food from passing currents by drawing water into their body and removing the food before eliminating the strained water. Some, such as black leather chitons, have specialized mouthparts for rasping algae and organic particles from underwater surfaces.

These creatures may also be predatory, actively hunting other animals on the ocean floor and in open water. Invertebrates such as lion's mane jellyfish capture small animals that blunder into their extended tentacles, which are armed with stinging cells.

The bottom line of survival for any animal is to find food without becoming food. Alaska's seashore creatures employ an array of techniques for avoiding predators. Some, such as hairy tritons, withdraw into the protection of a shell. Others, like seaweed isopods, hide under rocks or in crevices. Octopuses bite an enemy, jellyfish sting, and urchins use spines. Graceful kelp crabs camouflage themselves; brittle stars shed body parts. Others, such as scallops, simply flee confrontations.

CLASSIFYING THE CREATURES • All the
invertebrates featured in this book belong to the scientific kingdom known as Animalia. That is, they are animals, not plants.

The animal kingdom, like the plant kingdom, is divided into a great many classifications, determined by common biological characteristics. The broadest groupings are the large divisions known as phyla. Each phylum, in turn, is divided into classes, then into orders, and so on.

We arrive finally at the very specific level of classification known as genus and species. Each animal pictured in this guide is identified by its common name (for example, the blue mussel) and by its genus and species name (in this case, *Mytilus trossulus*). These Latin names, recognized around the world, are especially useful when common names cause confusion.

Following is an example of scientific classification for one of Alaska's common marine invertebrates, the red king crab (*Paralithodes camtschaticus*):

Kingdom: Animalia
Phylum: Arthropoda
Subphylum: Crustacea
Class: Malacostraca

Order: Decapoda
Suborder: Pleocyemata
Infraorder: Anomura
Superfamily: Paguroidea
Family: Lithodidae
Genus: *Paralithodes*
Species: *camtschaticus*

With this book as a guide, you'll be able to connect the names with some of the strange and remarkable seashore creatures you encounter along the Alaskan coast. We have explored the state's beaches for many years, watching how these animals live. Yet every time we walk along a shoreline, something new catches our attention—perhaps an unfamiliar animal or an unusual behavior. The thrill of spending time on a beach comes from that element of surprise: What will the ocean show us this time?

Red king crab

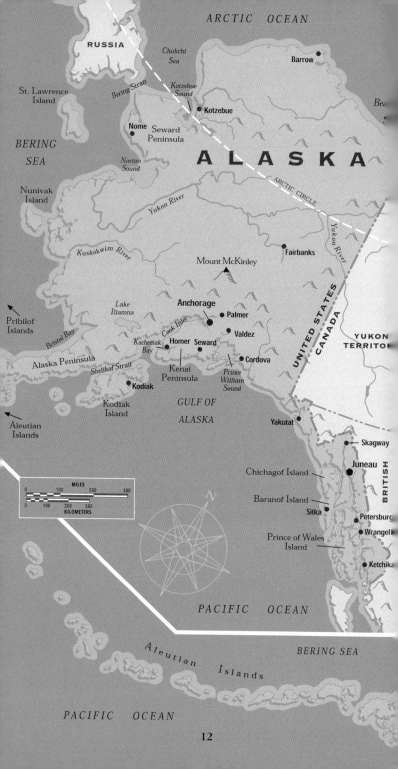

ARCTIC OCEAN

RUSSIA

Chukchi Sea

Bering Strait

Kotzebue Sound

● Kotzebue

● Barrow

St. Lawrence Island

● Nome

Seward Peninsula

BERING SEA

Norton Sound

A L A S K A

ARCTIC CIRCLE

Nunivak Island

Yukon River

Kuskokwim River

Yukon River

● Fairbanks

Mount McKinley ▲

Lake Iliamna

Anchorage ●

● Palmer

UNITED STATES

CANADA

YUKON TERRITOR

Pribilof Islands

Bristol Bay

Cook Inlet

● Valdez

Kachemak Bay Homer

Seward

Alaska Peninsula

Shelikof Strait

Kenai Peninsula

● Cordova

Prince William Sound

● Kodiak

Kodiak Island

GULF OF ALASKA

Aleutian Islands

● Yakutat

● Skagway

● Juneau

Chichagof Island

BRITISH

MILES

0   100   200   300

0   100   200   300

KILOMETERS

Baranof Island

Sitka ●

Prince of Wales Island

● Petersburg

● Wrangel

● Ketchika

N

PACIFIC OCEAN

Aleutian Islands

BERING SEA

PACIFIC OCEAN

Sponges

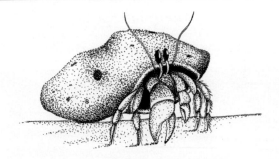

Deepwater sponges may look like fans, vases, or fingers, while sponges that encrust the undersides and crevices of rocks in the intertidal zone look like globs of colorful cookie dough.

Wandering sponges of Suberites species often colonize the shells of active hermit crabs.

A sponge's roughly textured surface is marked by numerous tiny pores into which water flows and by one or more larger openings from which water and waste products leave the sponge. All holes are connected by an internal system of canals and cavities lined with specialized cells. Each cell bears a whiplike appendage, and these appendages create a current that moves water throughout the animal. The cells filter the water, absorbing and digesting its nutrients.

The living portions of a sponge are soft and gelatinous, but the body is supported by a flexible skeleton of chalky, glassy, or protein particles. The skeletons of certain deepwater sponges become the commercial sponges sold for bathing.

Sponges possess the world's greatest power of regeneration. If fragments are broken off from a sponge, each piece can regrow, under favorable conditions, into a healthy new animal. Most sponges probably live 2 or 3 years, but some cold-water species may survive well past 50 years of age.

Sponges, having no nervous system, don't withdraw or change form when you touch them. Some sponges give off a pungent odor to discourage predators, which in Alaska include sea stars, chitons, and nudibranchs. Researchers collect sponges as sources of biochemical products associated with medicine.

Breadcrumb Sponge

Species of HALICHONDRIA

One of Alaska's most widespread encrusting sponges is the bread-crumb (or crumb-of-bread) sponge, whose habitat can include rock

Water from which food has been filtered leaves a sponge's body through the volcano-shaped holes.

undersides, kelp holdfasts, floating docks, pilings, and empty seashells. Breadcrumb sponges are found from the midintertidal zone out to a depth of more than 200 feet, and range from arctic Alaska to Baja California. These sponges are occasionally exposed during minus tides and can tolerate air and sun exposure better than species that live solely beyond the low-tide line.

Breadcrumb sponges are yellow or greenish yellow, the color influenced by the presence of microscopic marine plants (algae) responding to light. These sponges, bearing many volcano-like holes through which filtered water is expelled, conform to the contours of the surface they live on. Large colonies may be an inch thick and more than 3 feet wide.

Like their deepwater relatives, breadcrumb sponges lack distinct tissues and organs and are supported by a framework of interlaced, needlelike particles. This sponge's body commonly provides a refuge for other invertebrates—even species that prey on the sponge, most commonly the lemon peel and false lemon peel nudibranchs. A sponge on Alaska's coastline may harbor a small diversity of tenants.

Cnidarians

Cnidarians (pronounced nye-DARE-ee-ans) have a soft, hollow body and centrally located mouth fringed by tentacles armed with stinging cells. This group includes jellyfish, anemones, hydrozoans (or hydroids), sea pens, and corals.

Cnidarians, formerly known as coelenterates, are basically gelatinous sacs composed of two cellular layers separated by a jellylike layer. Some cnidarians display a bell-like, pulsating medusa form with trailing tentacles (jellyfish, for example), named for its resemblance to the snaky hairdo of Medusa, the mythological Gorgon. Other cnidarians, such as anemones, live as saclike blobs, or polyps, attached to boulders and other underwater objects or to man-made structures.

Some cnidarian species exhibit both the polyp and medusa forms during their life cycle. Certain types live as solitary individuals; others exist as colonies of animals.

Cnidarian tentacles are equipped with tiny capsules containing stinging cells called nematocysts. A coiled, hollow thread shoots out of a nematocyst to pierce or entangle whatever has touched the tentacle. The firing of a nematocyst's harpoon is a direct response to touch without input from the animal's nervous system. This explains why a person can be stung by a jellyfish without ever encountering a live one; even after it has died and washed ashore or its tentacles have broken into pieces at sea, it can deliver a painful reminder of its existence.

A cnidarian's prey is taken into the gut through its mouth, with indigestible remnants later expelled through the same opening. Most cnidarians are carnivores, preying on microscopic plankton, crabs, shrimps, isopods, amphipods, snails, sea stars, urchins, and fish.

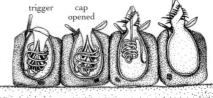

Nematocyst cells of a cnidarian: progression of barb being fired

trigger   cap opened

coiled nematocyst   fully extended nematocyst (fired)

JELLYFISH

Jellyfish—unrelated to fish despite their name—are plankton, drifting at the mercy of ocean currents in their search for food. The "jelly" of jellyfish is a thick gelatinous layer that separates the inner and outer cell layers of the body wall. Jellyfish bear tentacles, laden with stinging nematocysts, that extend from their body's margin.

A mouth hangs by a stalk from the center of the animal's underside. This stalk combines with the bell-shaped (or inverted-bowl-shaped) body to give the jelly a remarkable resemblance to a floating umbrella. Surrounding the mouth are frilly or flaplike oral lobes that may trail from a jelly's underside in great streaming ruffles and aid in food capture by means of additional nematocysts.

Jellyfish move with rhythmic pulsing of the bell. Contractions at the bell's margin force water out, creating a weak jet propulsion. Jellyfish are not strong swimmers; currents and waves move them horizontally, but they do have limited control over their vertical movement.

At the bell's margins are numerous light sensors and balancing organs. The sensors stimulate a jellyfish to move toward or away from light. The balancing organs trigger a righting reflex should a jelly become disoriented.

The best places for watching jellyfish pulse through the water in Alaska are from docks in coastal harbors and boats on open water.

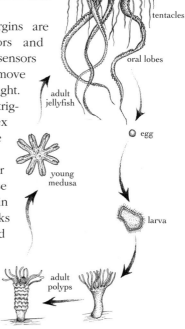

bell

tentacles

oral lobes

adult jellyfish

egg

young medusa

larva

adult polyps

Stages in development of some jellyfish

16

Lion's Mane Jellyfish

CYANEA CAPILLATA

Lion's mane jellyfish are the largest jellies in Alaskan waters. Roaming the Pacific Ocean from

In this view from the top, a lion's mane jellyfish displays its reddish interior.

arctic Alaska to Oregon, these giants can measure over 2 feet across the bell and can bear up to 150 tentacles that extend more than 8 feet beneath them.

Lion's mane jellies have a flattened bell with a thick center and a thinner, 8-lobed margin. The bell is generally translucent or milky white toward the margins. The bell's interior in younger individuals is usually reddish, eventually changing to a golden brown in maturity.

Eight groups of long tentacles hang below the bell's margin. In addition, 4 frilly and extendable oral lobes surround the mouth. Like the tentacles, these lobes have stinging cells that can cause severe rash or pain. Lion's mane jellyfish are the species most responsible for people being stung in Alaska.

This jellyfish lives for only about 1 year. A juvenile just an eighth of an inch wide can grow in a single summer into an adult over 2 feet wide. They eat almost anything that comes into contact with their armed tentacles: plankton, small fish, crabs, shrimps, nudibranchs, and some other jellyfish. They are preyed upon in turn by various anemones, nudibranchs, and shrimps, as well as being scavenged by sunflower stars.

SEA ANEMONES

Sea anemones are saclike creatures that usually remain permanently attached to hard surfaces. They prefer sites with substantial currents to provide them with adequate food.

An anemone's tubular body is specialized for a sedentary lifestyle. One end of the body forms a broad disk that sticks to a surface. It's virtually impossible to remove an attached anemone from its home without harming it.

Surprisingly, some anemones will occasionally detach themselves and somersault or creep to a better spot. This behavior is commonly witnessed in aquariums as newly introduced anemones try to find a suitable home.

At the opposite end of the body is the anemone's oral disk. Here lies the mouth, surrounded by one or more rows of tentacles armed with stinging cells. The tentacles may be fully extended when the anemone is feeding, giving it a flowery appearance.

Unlike the stinging tentacles of some jellyfish, those of Alaskan anemones don't sting humans. Tidepoolers who touch a tentacle will feel only a sticky sensation, the result of stinging cells that are too short or not toxic enough to cause harm. However, for small invertebrates and fish that blunder into the swaying tentacles, these weapons are deadly.

An anemone threatened by a predatory nudibranch or exposed by an ebbing tide may withdraw its tentacles into the body cavity. Then the anemone will look like a shiny blob or an indistinct ring of pebbles.

Christmas anemone
(Urticina
crassicornis)

Frilled Anemone

The largest and most familiar anemone in Alaska is the frilled anemone. From arctic Alaska to Southern California, they reside

Hundreds of food-trapping white tentacles extend from the body of this frilled anemone.

singly or in large groups on docks, boat hulls, kelp, or boulders on protected rocky shorelines. Up to a thousand finely branched tentacles extend from the animal's body, giving it a frilly appearance and its common name.

Frilled anemones are commonly opaque white, but individuals may be pink, orange, tan, or brown. They may also sport a two-toned look with a pink, orange, or brownish body and whitish tentacles. Large frilled anemones, most of which are the related *Metridum giganteum*, resemble feather dusters and can be over 3 feet tall. They are extremely long-lived, perhaps surviving for more than 100 years.

Frilled anemones are carnivores, trapping plankton and occasionally worms in their tentacles. In turn, they are preyed upon by maned nudibranchs and leather stars.

A submerged frilled anemone can release its grip on its home base and creep away at the rapid speed (for an anemone) of half an inch per hour. Another of its defense techniques is to discharge long white threads loaded with stinging cells from the mouth and tiny pores in the body wall.

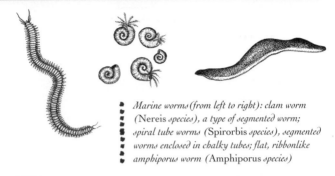

Marine worms (from left to right): clam worm (Nereis species), a type of segmented worm; spiral tube worms (Spirorbis species), segmented worms enclosed in chalky tubes; flat, ribbonlike amphiporus worm (Amphiporus species)

Worms, while found on beaches throughout the world, are not high-profile marine animals. Many Pacific coast worms, in fact, have yet to be described and named by researchers. However, they are valuable components of oceanic food webs and exhibit fascinating survival strategies.

Most seashore worms belong to one of three main groups: the flatworms, the ribbon worms, or the segmented worms.

Unlike their terrestrial relatives, marine flatworms are not parasitic on other animals. Flatworms have no body cavity; their organs are simply incorporated into the body tissues. Alaska's giant flatworm might be mistaken for a wet leaf or slimy growth of algae as it hunts under rocks for small invertebrates, including other flatworms.

Ribbon worms, also called nemertean worms, use muscular waves created by expanding or contracting sections of the body in order to move. They generally feed on other invertebrates, including other worms.

Oceanic segmented worms are also called polychaete worms—derived from the Greek *poly* for "much" and *chaite* for "hair." This name refers to the bristles along a worm's side. Polychaete worms possess an advanced means of locomotion compared with other types of worms. Fleshy outgrowths, some of them bearing bundles of bristles, extend from the animal's sides. The bristles increase traction as the worm contracts and elongates its segments, creating muscular waves that pass down the body.

Polychaete worms eat other invertebrates and algae.

Red Ribbon Worm

▲▼▲■▼▲▲▼▲■▲▼▲▲▼▲■▲▼▲▲▼▲■▲▼▲▲▼▲

TUBULANUS POLYMORPHUS

Red ribbon worms live under rocks and seaweed or among mussel and barnacle beds from Southcentral Alaska to Southern

A red ribbon worm can give the appearance of a tangled knot. These worms grow to lengths of over 3 feet.

California. A red ribbon worm is uniformly bright red, orange, or maroon in color. It secretes a slime layer on which to glide.

The worm's soft body is basically a ribbon of smooth muscle encasing a tubular gut, with mouth and anus at opposite ends. The mouth is a long slit on the underside of the worm's indistinct head. Ribbon worms possess a long tonguelike organ that shoots out of a pore near the mouth to capture prey on a sticky or barbed tip.

Most active at night, these worms are "armchair hunters," lying fairly immobile in a protected site and simply extending their feeding organ to snare prey.

Red ribbon worms are especially noteworthy for their ability to regenerate entire animals from body fragments. One worm can be cut into dozens of thin slices, and each will develop into a new individual. This remarkable adaptation makes killing a ribbon worm very difficult for predators.

Scale Worm

Scale worms live in kelp holdfasts and mussel beds and on undersides of rocks from Southcentral Alaska to Baja California. These segmented worms are found from

The mottled scales covering this worm's body can be shed—and later regenerated—if the worm is threatened.

the midintertidal zone out to a depth of almost 1,800 feet.

This worm's most obvious feature is the set of oval-shaped, overlapping scales that cover its back in two rows, forming a protective armor against attack. The scales are generally mottled brown or gray, while the worm's underside and the upper body surface (sometimes visible between the scales) is whitish or yellowish white.

Some scale worms are free-living. Others settle down to a commensal relationship with a specific host, which provides the worm with protection and a free ride but neither harms nor benefits the host. This scale worm has been seen living commensally with larger segmented worms, molluscs, and sea stars. Most free-living scale worms are 1 to 2 inches long, but their commensal counterparts can grow to lengths of over 4 inches.

Their diet includes organic particles and a variety of marine invertebrates—including other scale worms. Their strong, four-jawed mouthpart can rip off scales or tear pieces from the end of another worm's body. When harassed, scale worms can shed scales or roll into a ball.

Cone Worm

PECTINARIA GRANULATA

Cone worms, also known as ice cream cone or sandmason worms, live in sandy areas from Western Alaska to Puget Sound, Washington. Most people would overlook

Cone worms build long, tapered tubes of even-sized sand grains, the finished wall being a single layer of quartz granules.

this little 1½-inch-long segmented worm were it not for the remarkable home it constructs to provide protection from predators.

To build its conical house of sand, the worm picks up each quartz grain with its mouth and touches it to a cement gland on its body before adding the new building block to the tube. This process continues throughout its life.

The only visible part of the worm itself is a set of brilliant golden bristles at the wide end of the tube, functioning both as digging appendages and trapdoors for keeping predators out. Below the bristles are feathery tentacles that carry food-laden sand to the worm's mouth. Cone worms dig through and ingest sand or sandy mud for any organic particles it might contain.

The wide end of the cone points down into the sand, with the animal living head down in the tube, constantly shoveling material into its mouth. The narrow end of the cone projects just above the ocean floor, allowing processed sand and other waste products to be expelled.

23

Molluscs

Molluscs are an immense group of terrestrial and aquatic invertebrates with more than 100,000 species worldwide. Marine molluscs have a wide range of habitats—from the splash zone above

Examples of molluscan groups (left to right): lined chiton; arms of common Pacific octopus; spotted nudibranch; puppet margarite; Nuttall's cockle

the high-tide line to incredible depths on the ocean floor. Familiar molluscs among the two dozen pictured in this guide include chitons, gastropods (such as snails and nudibranchs), bivalves (such as mussels and clams), and cephalopods (the octopus).

Most molluscs create a shell to protect their soft body. A few molluscs—such as octopuses, nudibranchs, and naked sea butterflies—lack a shell as adults and depend on means of protection different from those of their armored relatives. Molluscs never shed one shell for another; an empty shell indicates the death of its original owner. A mollusc's shell is usually more familiar to seashore visitors than the animal itself.

Unique to molluscs is the mantle, a fold of soft, thickened flesh encasing the internal organs and specialized gills. The mantle secretes the shell, producing layers of calcium carbonate and organic chemicals.

Mollusc bodies are divided into three main regions: the head, foot, and guts. The head contains sensory organs and a mouth in all molluscs except the bivalves. Within the mouth a rasping tongue called the radula bears from one to thousands of tiny teeth. The foot is a muscle used for crawling, swimming, or burrowing. The visceral mass—the guts—is the main part of the body, consisting of respiratory, circulatory, digestive, excretory, and reproductive organs.

Chitons

Chitons (pronounced KYE-tuns) are well-armored animals that inhabit rocky shorelines throughout the world. A chiton's flattened oval body is covered by a shell composed of 8 overlapping plates firmly embedded into the animal's flesh by muscles and ligaments.

The plates may display one or more solid colors or an intricate design of many colors. Only gumboot chitons, their plates buried within the tough flesh, lack the chiton's typical armadillo-like appearance.

When a chiton dies and its soft parts decompose, the shell pieces (often bleached by the sun at the high-tide line) are referred to as butterfly shells. A number of Alaskan artists create jewelry, especially earrings, from these marine treasures.

Chitons are sluggish creatures that generally avoid light and remain lethargic during the day. At night, however, submerged chitons scour their surroundings, using their rasping tongue to scrape diatoms, algal films, and organic particles from the rocks. Some chitons also eat bryozoans, small worms, or, rarely, small shrimps.

A chiton will often reside at a distinct resting spot, or homing area. Its large foot and its girdle—that portion of its upper surface surrounding the protective plates—will clamp down tightly to a surface, securing the animal against crashing waves and strong currents. Suction created by the foot makes the animal nearly impossible to remove.

Adhering tenaciously to rock is a chiton's main defense against predators like fish, crabs, sea stars, and humans. If it should somehow be removed, it will roll into a ball, its plates serving to shield the edible underside.

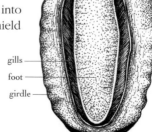

mouth

gills

foot

girdle

Underside of a black leather chiton

25

Black Leather Chiton

KATHARINA TUNICATA

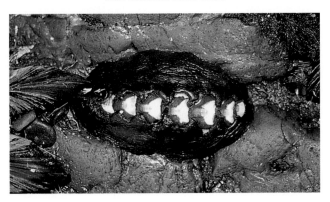

The black leather, or black Katy, chiton is a common inhabitant of middle to lower intertidal zones from Kamchatka, Russia, and Alaska's Aleutian Islands to Southern California. Though found in both protected and exposed sites, this hardy chiton prefers shores where strong wave action and currents prevail.

Surrounded by blue mussels and anchored by suction, this black leather chiton waits for the rising tide to resume feeding.

These chitons are aptly named. Their smooth, shiny black girdles, reaching lengths of nearly 5 inches and covering about two-thirds of each protective plate, look and feel like wet leather. Only a small, diamond-shaped portion of each of the 8 plates is visible, these being blackish or gray. Various marine organisms are frequently found attached to the exposed part of the plates.

The large foot is usually dull orange or yellowish, bordered by a row of gills on each side. A black leather chiton may reach 3 years of age.

This animal is unusual among the chitons for its relative insensitivity to light, actively feeding both day and night on brown and red algae, as well as on growths of microscopic marine plants called diatoms. Black leather chitons have long been a traditional Native food in Alaska and can be eaten raw or boiled, or added to chowders. Sea stars also prey on these chitons.

Gumboot Chiton

CRYPTOCHITON STELLERI

Gumboot chitons, usually reddish in color, take their common name from the animal's resemblance to the rubber, or gum, boots worn *This 8-inch-long gumboot chiton may grow to measure 12 inches long and live more than 20 years.* by Alaska's coastal residents. This species prefers protected rocky shorelines from Western Alaska to Southern California.

Three features make gumboots unique among chitons. The first is their sheer size—commonly over a foot long, making them the world's largest chitons. The second is a lack of exposed plates on the animal's upper surface. Large, butterfly-shaped plates are covered by the chiton's flesh, though bulges in the creature's outline reveal their presence. Third, this species does not cling tightly to rocks when exposed and so can be easily dislodged, often washing ashore during storms.

Sensitive to light, gumboots are nocturnal grazers and prefer to remain on rocks below the low-tide line or cling to the undersides of intertidal rocks during daylight hours. These animals, feeding primarily on red algae, don't travel far. In one study, marked individuals remained within 66 feet of their release site even after 2 years.

The gumboot's large golden foot historically was valued as a food source by Russian settlers and is still harvested by coastal Natives.

GASTROPODS

About three-quarters of the world's molluscs belong to a group known as the gastropods, a word that means "stomach-foot." Their flattened muscular foot, adapted for creeping, lies adjacent to the stomach.

Marine gastropods include abalones, limpets, snails (such as periwinkles, moon snails, tritons, and dogwinkles), and nudibranchs. All have a distinct head with simple eyes that detect light, a mouth bearing a rasping tongue, and 2 or more retractable tentacles.

Shell of a ridged neptune (Neptunea lyrata)

Many gastropods live on plant material, using their tooth-laden tongue to graze algae off hard surfaces. Others are carnivores with specialized mouthparts to kill their prey.

Gastropod shells consist of a single piece, hence another name for the group: the univalves (meaning "one shell"). The shell is very obvious in some species, but in others it is present only in the microscopic young animal.

Snails with their shells coiled into tight spirals are the most familiar gastropods to Alaska's beachcombers. Snails start out life on the ocean floor with a shell no bigger than the very tip of their adult shell. New chalky material is added throughout their lifetime (generally 5 years or less).

Some snail (and bivalve) shells bear a thin, outer protein layer called the periostracum. This covering, secreted by the mollusc itself, is usually tan or brownish and provides camouflage, protects the shell against erosion, or reduces friction as the animal moves through a substrate.

Each horizontal section of a snail's shell is called a whorl, with the newest, lowermost one—the body whorl—containing most of the animal's soft parts. When the snail is feeding or on the move, its head and foot typically extend outside the shell. If threatened, it can withdraw into the shell, sealing the opening with a trapdoor plate attached to the foot.

ABALONES • Abalones have flattened shells and lack a protective trapdoor. Most of the shell is composed of the body whorl, and its border is characterized by a row of holes through which filtered water and waste products are released.

Northern Abalone

HALIOTIS KAMTSCHATKANA

Alaska's only abalone, the northern or pinto abalone, forages along exposed outer coasts from

This abalone shell's reddish exterior is due to a diet of brown and red algae.

Southeast Alaska to Southern California, scraping microscopic plants from rocks and eating pieces of loose algae.

This abalone can measure over 6 inches long and has a distinctive ear-shaped, wavy shell—usually mottled red and green, with 3 to 6 open holes along one margin. A clutter of organisms often lives on an abalone's shell.

If attacked by a sea star, an abalone can extend its body outside the shell to dislodge the predator's tube feet. Or the abalone can try to shake the star off by rotating the shell back and forth in a wide arc. An abalone can also flee predators, crawling away at speeds of up to 10 inches per minute. Or it can use the suction—up to 4,000 times its body weight—created by its foot to clamp onto rocks.

Humans value the shell's pearly interior, used in making jewelry, and the animal's large edible foot. Alaskan abalones that avoid predation by bottom fish, crabs, sea otters, and sea stars may live 20 years or more.

LIMPETS • Limpets have tent-shaped shells and no trapdoor. They are popularly called "Chinese hats" because of their resemblance to Asian straw hats.

Plate Limpet

TECTURA SCUTUM

One of Alaska's most familiar seashore creatures is the plate limpet. Measuring to about 2½ inches long, they are found on rocks and algae in relatively shallow

Plate limpets routinely visit one specific site while the tide is out, anchoring themselves with suction from a muscular foot.

water or on floating docks and pilings from Western Alaska to Southern California.

The flattened oval shell is usually gray, brown, or olive, with lighter blotches or streaks arranged as a checkerboard pattern or as radiating lines of color.

The animal's body is whitish yellow or dull gold. Having no trapdoor to retreat behind, the foot and head with tentacles are visible if the limpet is removed from its place of attachment. Limpets use the tenacity of their grip for protection, attaching firmly to hard surfaces when exposed by an ebbing tide or threatened by a potential predator.

Limpets are primarily nocturnal and tend to follow the water up and down intertidal rocks as the tide comes in and goes out. These herbivores graze algae and organic particles from a surface with their long rasping tongue. Predators include shorebirds, seabirds, and sea stars.

PERIWINKLES • Periwinkles are small grazing snails with drab-colored roundish or spindle-shaped shells. Capable of withstanding the hardships of high-intertidal-zone life, periwinkles need only wet their gills occasionally and can fast for long periods of time.

Sitka Periwinkle

LITTORINA SITKANA

Ranging from Western Alaska to Puget Sound, Washington, these ¾-inch-high snails wear a fat shell that is blackish gray or dark brown. Alternating dark and yellowish (or white-gray) bands are common.

The sculpture and color of these shells vary greatly between individuals, but the snail inside is black in color.

On shorelines with moderate surf, these snails may live within the splash zone above the high-tide line. They also are found among acorn barnacles from the high-tide line down to the midintertidal zone. At lower reaches of a beach, what may look like a mass of periwinkles under a rock is more likely to be a group of hermit crabs living in secondhand periwinkle shells.

An exposed Sitka periwinkle can survive long periods of exposure by trapping moisture within its shell. The snail withdraws into its shell, closing the trapdoor, and mucus produced by the foot hardens along the shell's opening, forming a tight seal.

Sea stars and anemones eat Sitka periwinkles.

MOON SNAILS • Moon snails are carnivorous snails of Alaska's soft-bottomed shorelines. Their empty round shells may be found cast ashore on beaches along-side shells of molluscs that they've eaten.

Aleutian Moon Snail

NATICA ALEUTICA

Aleutian moon snails are incon-spicuous residents of sand, mud, or gravel shorelines from arctic *This snail uses its speckled white and maroon foot to plow through sandy mud.* Alaska to Southeast Alaska. Their light brown or brownish pink shells can measure 2½ inches high.

When the snail retreats into its shell, it seals the open-ing with a chalky white or grayish white trapdoor. The body of the snail itself is cream-colored with rusty red or maroon blotches.

These snails, found from the low intertidal zone out to a depth of almost 1,500 feet, feed on clams, snails, and dead fish. A moon snail uses its strong foot to displace and grasp clams. Then, employing its rasping tongue and a shell-softening secretion, it drills a hole through the shell and sucks out the clam's soft tissue. In turn, moon snails are eaten by sunflower stars, other moon snails, and bottom fish.

The Aleutian moon snail female lays thousands of tiny white eggs in spring or summer within a wide, curving sheet of mucus embedded with sand grains. This smooth "sand collar" usually forms an overlapping circle.

TRITONS • Tritons are large, heavy-shelled snails that prey on other invertebrates.

Hairy Triton

FUSITRITON OREGONENSE

Hairy tritons range from the Bering Sea and Aleutian Islands to Baja California. These giants can be almost 6 inches high and 3 inches wide. While preferring sites in

Stretching its fleshy foot and attached trapdoor, a hairy triton attempts to right itself after being flipped by a crab.

water depths of over 1,700 feet, tritons may be encountered on intertidal rocks, mud, or sand.

The shell's thin outer covering—composed of brownish, spirally arranged bristles—gives this snail a hairy appearance and its common name. The elongated shell is adorned with a checkerboard pattern of raised ribs—most evident on surf-worn empty shells. The triton's body is pinkish yellow and mottled with maroon or black. The shell's opening, exhibiting a white interior, can be sealed by a thick brown trapdoor of horny material.

Hairy tritons are aggressive carnivores, boring a hole into the outer covering of clams, urchins, and sea squirts and then feeding on their prey's soft parts. They also scavenge dead organisms from the ocean floor.

In the spring and early summer, females deposit a compact spiral of sturdy egg capsules on rock surfaces, each capsule resembling a translucent kernel of corn.

33

DOGWINKLES • Alaska's dog-winkle snails are commonly found on rocks or among mussels in the shoreline's middle and lower intertidal zones. Ranging from Western Alaska to Central California are the frilled dogwinkle and 3 very similar smaller species: the channeled, the emarginate, and the file dogwinkles.

The robust spindle-shaped shells of these smaller dogwinkles are 1 to 2 inches long and of a solid or banded coloration ranging from brownish green to whitish orange. Subtle differences make it possible to distinguish between the 3 species.

The segments, or whorls, of a channeled dogwinkle's shell peak in a tall spire and bear spiraling raised cords of relatively equal size that are separated by deep, narrow grooves.

An emarginate dogwinkle's similarly shaded shell has a lower spire and heavy raised cords alternating with more delicate ones, all of which are closely spaced.

A file dogwinkle's shell is intermediate in appearance between its two relatives, exhibiting a low spire with heavily pronounced or fine spiral cords.

Dogwinkles prey heavily on barnacles and blue mussels. A

The shells of 3 dogwinkle species (from top to bottom): channeled dogwinkle (Nucella canaliculata); emarginate dogwinkle (Nucella marginata); and file dogwinkle (Nucella lima)

dogwinkle will spend a day or two drilling into and consuming its prey. Individuals of some species also eat limpets and small grazing snails, as well as snail eggs (even eggs of their own kind).

Dogwinkles are known as the dye snails, for a gland that secretes a purple substance. This secretion, when ground up with the snail's body, produces a dull violet dye that has been used historically by North American Indians.

Frilled Dogwinkle

NUCELLA LAMELLOSA

Frilled dogwinkles, also called wrinkled dog whelks or wrinkled purple snails, are medium-size snails that inhabit low intertidal and shallow subtidal rocks from *The frills running length-wise down these dogwinkle shells are rather worn, perhaps due to life on a surf-swept, exposed beach.* the Bering Sea to the Pacific around Central California. They prefer crevices or sheltered sites within mussel and barnacle beds.

Frilled dogwinkle shells, reaching 3½ inches in height, are adorned with smooth, raised, spiraling ridges and vertical frilly outgrowths. Both ridges and frills sometimes exist as only subtle lines running perpendicular to each other, especially in exposed locations.

Frilled dogwinkle shells can be white, tan, orangish brown, gray, or purple, sometimes with spiral banding as well. The shell's opening, sealed by the animal with a horny trapdoor, is oval with a yellowish interior and bordered by a white, flared lip sporting 3 rounded teeth.

Frilled dogwinkles are efficient predators of acorn barnacles and blue mussels. They force open a barnacle's top plates or drill through a mussel's shell to get at the edible soft parts. They also eat sea squirts.

Female frilled dogwinkles deposit dense clusters of vase-shaped egg capsules called sea oats. Crabs and fish prey heavily on developing larvae.

NUDIBRANCHS • Nudibranchs (pronounced NEW-duh-branks) are gastropods with no shell. Larval forms possess a shell that is lost later in the animal's development.

Some nudibranchs incorporate the bad tastes or lethal traits of their prey into their own bodies, thus presenting an unsavory meal to potential attackers. Bright colors may warn predators of the potential for poisonous stings or a foul taste.

Orange-tipped Nudibranch

TRIOPHA CATALINAE

The orange-tipped nudibranch is a resident of tidepools, kelp beds, and floating docks from Western Alaska to Baja California. Its almost

The nudibranch's head (top of photo) bears two thick, orange tentacles that serve as sensory organs.

cylindrical, bright white body is adorned with scattered orange-tipped bumps. Its hind end bears a ring of 5 non-retractable white plumes, or gills, tipped in orange.

The arrangement of orange projections on the animal's broad head resemble a face, giving this species the additional name of clown nudibranch.

Orange-tipped nudibranchs feed primarily on bryozoans living in or below the midintertidal zone. They scrape these microscopic animals from rocks or algae with their specialized tongue, digesting the soft parts internally. Only inexperienced fish, or possibly other nudibranchs, are known to eat orange-tipped nudibranchs.

False Lemon Peel Nudibranch

ARCHIDORIS MONTEREYENSIS

This fairly large, oval-shaped nudibranch ranges from South-central Alaska to Southern California, and is found from the low intertidal zone out to depths of over 800 feet. The animal, especially when it's not submerged, resembles an old lemon peel. Its plump, warty-looking body is light to vivid yellow or orangish yellow and can measure almost 6 inches long.

A ring of feathery gills projects from this nudibranch's hind (lower left) end. The word "nudibranch" means "naked gill."

Usually scattered along the upper surface of the body are dark gray or black blotches. These spots are found both on and between the yellow knobby bumps covering the animal's back. This characteristic separates the false lemon peel from its look-alike relative, the sea lemon (*Anisodoris nobilis*), which bears blackish spots only between the bumps, not on top of them.

The false lemon peel nudibranch displays a ring of 7 retractable yellow gills on the hind end of its body. A pair of thick comblike tentacles rises up from the body's forward region.

To find these nudibranchs, locate their food: encrusting sponges, especially breadcrumb sponges. The nudibranch may barely be distinguishable from its prey.

Few, if any, marine animals are known to prey on this species.

Opalescent Nudibranch

HERMISSENDA CRASSICORNIS

Discovering an opalescent nudi-branch can be the highlight of a day's outing at the seashore for Alaskan tidepoolers. Out of water

This striking inch-long nudibranch crawls forward as it searches for a meal of hydroids or anemones.

this nudibranch is a shapeless blob, but submerged it becomes an image of graceful beauty. From Southcentral Alaska to Baja California, these nudibranchs live in the low intertidal and subtidal zones among rocks, on mudflats, on floating docks, and in eelgrass beds.

Opalescent nudibranchs can be over 2 inches in length. An opalescent nudibranch's translucent white body has a brilliant orange centerline and several electric-blue lateral stripes running the length of it. The animal has an orange and white waving fringe of fleshy, tapering projections called cerata on its upper surface.

Opalescent nudibranchs are aggressive predators that can eat stinging invertebrates, such as anemones and hydroids, without triggering the harpoonlike barbs contained in their prey's stinging cells.

These barbs pass from the nudibranch's stomach to extensions of the digestive tract in the tips of the cerata. When harassed, the nudibranch will toss these projections forward to warn of its potential for harming the invader, much like a porcupine will raise its quills forward when threatened.

BIVALVES

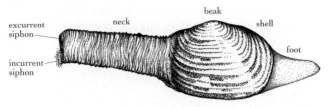

Bivalve molluscs include mussels, scallops, and clams. Bivalves (meaning "two shells") have a *A truncated mya is an example of a burrowing bivalve.* two-part shell formed by valves that hinge together along the top of the animal and surround its soft parts.

A prominent beak lies adjacent to the shell's hinge on its outer surface. The very tip of this beak was the animal's shell during its first year of life. The 2 valves are drawn and held together by 1 or 2 strong muscles that are anchored to both inner surfaces of the shells. When a bivalve dies and its soft parts are eaten or decompose, scars left on the shell's inner surfaces by these muscles are indicative of a particular species.

Bivalves have no head or rasping tongue like the snails. The hind end of a bivalve often bears a pair of siphons—tubular extensions of the body tissue. One siphon draws food and oxygen-rich water into the body cavity; the other expels filtered water and waste products. Clams typically hide by burrowing beneath the sand, mud, or gravel, and then extend the siphons upward in order to reach water.

Gills of a bivalve serve the dual purpose of extracting oxygen from the water for respiration and of collecting microscopic food from the water.

Some bivalves, such as mussels and rock oysters, remain attached by strong threads to intertidal rocks for their entire life. Others burrow into the substrate with a well-developed foot. Scallops use jet propulsion to move.

MUSSELS • Mussels are one of the most common and recognizable invertebrates on Alaska's shorelines and may be found anchored to rocks, pilings, dock floats, or other shells. Lacking siphons, they feed by means of mucus-covered gills that collect and transport food entering the mantle cavity when the shell is agape.

Blue Mussel

MYTILUS TROSSULUS

Blue mussels are common residents of beaches from arctic Alaska to Baja California. They sometimes form extensive beds in the high or midintertidal zones

Blue mussels permanently attach themselves to rock— and to each other—by means of strong connectors called byssal threads.

along rocky shores. Blue mussels can also be found in smaller concentrations near and below the low-tide line.

Growing to about 3 inches, this mussel has a slender brown foot and a blue, wedge-shaped shell with a pearly white or gray interior. A shiny dark purple or brown protein layer covers the elongated shell, giving it a blue-black appearance. Concentric growth rings are visible on the outer surface.

Blue mussels are eaten by sea stars, snails, crabs, fish, otters, beluga whales, coyotes, bears, gulls, crows, black oystercatchers, harlequin ducks, bald eagles, and humans. This species is an important cultivated bivalve in Alaska.

SCALLOPS • Scallops characteristically have a fan-shaped shell with waved (or scalloped) margins. They live unattached in areas where their main food source, plankton, is plentiful. To move they create a jet propulsion by forcing water through an opening near the shell's hinge and rapidly clapping the two valves together.

Spiny Scallop

CHLAMYS HASTATA

Spiny scallops are medium-size bivalves that range from the Aleutian Islands to Southern California. They live near or below
A spiny scallop, like most scallops, bears unequal wings (or ears) on either side of the shell's hinge.

the low-tide line on protected sandy, muddy, or rocky beaches and grow to a length of 2½ inches or more.

One of the two halves of the hinged shell is covered with about 20 to 24 prominent ribs radiating from the beak. The other half has only about half as many ribs as its counterpart, with fainter cords between these, and bears tiny arched spines, hence this creature's common name.

The pink, white, brownish red, or yellow shell has a much brighter interior than exterior.

While resting or feeding, a scallop's shell is usually partially open to allow food-rich water to come in contact with its mucus-covered gills (scallops don't have siphons).

Rays and sea stars prey on these scallops, and divers harvest them for their single tasty muscle.

JINGLE SHELLS • Jingle shells are recognized by their misshapen oysterlike shells with smooth, pearly interiors. They anchor themselves permanently to hard surfaces by means of strong threads that extend through a hole in the animal's lower shell.

Pacific Rock Oyster

PODODESMUS MACROSCHISMA

The Pacific rock oyster is not an oyster but has in common with its namesake a distorted shell. The animal's bright orange flesh is protected by a nearly circular, very flat, gray or whitish green shell that can measure over 3 inches long. The smaller and thinner half of the shell has a pear-shaped hole.

This shell's coarse exterior contrasts with a smooth, pearly interior (green due to minute green algae that live there).

The shell's outer surface has coarse, irregular radiating ribs and a few barely visible concentric growth lines. Rock oysters do not have siphons; their sticky gills collect plankton when the shell is open. They live in the low intertidal zone or deeper water, clinging to rocks, shells, pilings, and dock floats along much of Alaska's coastline.

The Pacific rock oyster is also called the Alaska or Pacific false jingle shell. They are often used to make wind chimes, mobiles, and earrings. Each shell has unique deformities and bears decorative remains from encrusting organisms, such as bryozoans or tube worms.

COCKLES • Cockles, sometimes called heart clams, have sturdy heart-shaped shells (that is, when the two valves of a shell are closed and then viewed from the side). A cockle's siphons are quite short, so it cannot burrow as deeply as most clams to escape predators.

Nuttall's Cockle

CLINOCARDIUM NUTTALLII

Nuttall's cockles are residents of the intertidal zone and of subtidal depths to about 90 feet from Western Alaska to Southern

Flattened ribs, separated by deep grooves, radiate from the cockle shell's beak to the margin.

California. Their large, roundish shells are brownish and covered by a very thin tan or yellowish protein layer. About 35 evenly spaced, flattened ribs are intersected by concentric growth lines.

This clam's very short siphons, resembling holes in the mantle rather than tubes, are fringed and often speckled. The animals burrow 1 to 3 inches into mud, sand, or fine gravel. They seem to prefer eelgrass mudflats.

Nuttall's cockles can reach lengths of almost 6 inches and ages of 7 to 15 years. Sea stars, sea otters, and various fish eat Nuttall's cockles, and they are harvested by humans for chowder.

The cockle's long, powerful foot enables it to leap across the ocean floor, escaping predators.

LARGE BURROWING CLAMS • The Pacific coast's large burrowing clams have in common their remarkable efficiency at excavating a home in which to live. They easily dig into mud, sand, or gravel to avoid predators, as well as to firmly secure themselves for filtering food from the water above. Because these clams possess a relatively large and edible foot, they are frequently sought by humans for food.

Pacific Surf Clam

MACTROMERIS POLYNYMA

The Pacific surf clam inhabits the low intertidal zone and near-shore waters of flat, surf-swept, sandy beaches from arctic Alaska to Puget Sound, Washington. Pacific surf clams attain a maximum width of about 5½ inches.

Fine concentric lines can be seen beneath the thin, brown protein layer coating the outside of this shell.

The shell's exterior is chalky white, and beneath a thin protein layer that is brown, olive, or yellowish are fine concentric lines spanning the length of the smooth, triangular shell. Because of their short siphons, these clams are found burrowed into sand or sandy gravel just below the surface.

Predators of these clams include sea otters and sunflower stars. Considered tough, though tasty, they are also eaten by people. Their large shells serve as ashtrays, soap dishes, or trinket holders in many Alaskan homes.

Pacific Gaper

TRESUS CAPAX

The Pacific gaper, a giant among Alaska's clams, can be found in quiet waters from Southcentral Alaska to Central California. Some-

The exterior of a gaper shell displays concentric growth lines and a slightly offset beak.

times referred to as a horse clam, it can weigh nearly 4 pounds and have a shell more than 8 inches wide.

The thick oval shell, rounded at the forward end, is white or gray and partially covered by a dark, brittle protein layer that is often worn off an empty shell.

The long, fused siphons, or neck, are covered by a leathery skin and cannot be fully pulled into the clam's shell. The gaping end from which the neck extends gives this clam its common name. Other names for the gaper include horseneck, rubberneck, or bigneck clam.

Pacific gapers inhabit protected beaches of sand, muddy sand, or gravel, where they burrow 18 to 36 inches. When exposed by an ebbing tide, a gaper may expel water from its retracting siphons in a fountain 2 or 3 feet high. Big individuals are sometimes confused with the larger Pacific geoduck (pronounced GOO-ee-duck), a clam that reaches its northernmost limit of sizable populations near Gustavus in Southeast Alaska.

Besides being preyed upon by humans for chowder and fish bait, gapers are eaten by moon snails, sea stars, sea otters, brown bears, Pacific halibut, and rays.

Pacific Razor Clam

SILIQUA PATULA

Pacific razor clams, found on exposed sandy beaches from Western Alaska to Central California, have flat, glossy brown or olive green shells with a character-

A glossy brown protein layer covers the outside of this shell. This layer is often partially worn off by waves and sand.

istic oblong shape. Their appearance might remind one of a straight razor, hence the common name.

The rather fragile shell, 5 to 7 inches wide in large specimens, does not cover the entire animal. When empty, the shell exhibits a shiny, whitish purple interior divided by a prominent vertical rib.

On surf-swept sandy or sandy mud beaches, razor clams burrow just below the surface and extend their short siphons to feed. A dimple of sand forms over the siphons when they are exposed by the receding tide, making razors easy to find when you are beachcombing or clamming on a minus tide.

Catching a razor clam is another matter. They avoid predators such as brown bears, sea otters, flounders, and clam diggers by extending their wedge-shaped foot down into the sand, enlarging this appendage to form an anchor and then pulling themselves toward it. Razors can escape vertically into the sand or mud at speeds of an inch a second for 18 seconds. These clams may live as long as 19 years.

Pacific Littleneck Clam

PROTOTHACA STAMINEA

Pacific littleneck clams, or steam-
ers as they are commonly called,
are abundant residents of protected sandy or muddy gravel
beaches from Western Alaska to

*A Pacific littleneck shell's
offset beak (umbo) and
intersecting horizontal and
vertical lines differentiate it
from similar bivalves.*

Baja California. Adults can be as small as 1 inch in width,
though they typically grow to somewhat over 2 inches wide.

The shell's checkerboard pattern, created by intersecting horizontal and vertical lines spanning its length, makes
for ready identification of the littleneck clam. The shell's
beak is usually offset toward one end and exhibits 3 distinct interlocking teeth on the inner surface.

The outside of the shell ranges in color from white or
gray to a rusty brown; some specimens have a mottled
appearance. Their short siphons, from which this species
got the name littleneck, are fused.

Pacific littlenecks—also known as hard-shelled clams,
rock clams, or ribbed carpet clams—are commercially
important and a favorite among clam connoisseurs.
Littlenecks are easy to find and harvest because they burrow only 4 to 8 inches below the surface.

Adults may reach maximum size at 10 years of age.
Marine predators of littleneck clams include various sea
stars, octopuses, moon snails, and sea otters.

Butter Clam

■▲●▶◀▲▶▲▶▲●▲▶◀▲▶▲●▲▶◀▲▶▲●▲▶◀▲▶▲●▲▶◀▲●

SAXIDOMUS GIGANTEUS

Butter clams are one of the most commonly found clams on beaches from Western Alaska to Central California. This animal prefers protected sandy or muddy gravel beaches at or below the low intertidal zone.

A butter clam shell's concentric growth rings reveal seasonal fluctuations in food, with winter shortages of plankton creating thinner rings.

Butter clams can reach maximum size in 6 to 8 years, with large individuals measuring over 5 inches wide. The thick, somewhat chalky shell has an offset beak and is elliptical, gaping open slightly at one end.

Well-defined concentric lines spanning the length of the white, gray, or tan shell can be used to estimate the animal's age, much like growth rings on a tree trunk cross section; these clams may live well over 20 years.

Butter clams have relatively short, black-tipped siphons. Older individuals, bearing longer siphons than juveniles, may burrow a foot or more into the ocean floor, while younger clams are found closer to the surface.

These clams are eaten by sea stars, moon snails, sea otters, walrus, and gulls. Large butter clams are prized for chowders by both commercial and recreational clammers.

Butter clams do not always spawn on an annual or even a regular basis, so care must be taken not to eliminate a local population by harvesting too many.

MACOMAS • Macomas are small, inconspicuous clams that inhabit gravel and mud beaches. Their shells are typically light colored. Macomas have two long, separate siphons, the incurrent siphon being used to vacuum organic debris that has settled onto the ocean floor.

A macoma feeding

Baltic Macoma

MACOMA BALTHICA

Baltic macomas live in the mud of quiet bays between arctic Alaska and Southern California. Surviving well at sites flushed continually with freshwater, they are common in estuaries and can occasionally be found inland in rivers.

These small pink clams are an important food source for shorebirds and water-fowl migrating and nesting along Alaska's coast.

The delicate oval, pink or sometimes yellowish shell of this species is generally less than an inch wide and bears fine concentric growth lines and a very thin and ragged tan protein layer.

The animal's two long, translucent white siphons can measure up to 10 times the length of the shell. In quiet pools the siphons may resemble small white worms. Large Baltic macomas burrow as deep as 12 inches into the mud. Baltic macomas are eaten by various coastal birds, six-rayed stars, and moon snails. These clams are often monitored for heavy metals in petroleum pollution studies.

SOFT-SHELLED CLAMS • Soft-shelled clams prefer to live in the mud of relatively shallow waters. Their chalky white shells, covered by a brownish protein layer, are fairly delicate—hence their common name—and often gape open at one or both ends. These clams filter huge amounts of water as they feed, with as much as a quart of water per hour passing through a single clam's body.

Truncated Mya

MYA TRUNCATA

Truncated myas are mud dwellers found from arctic Alaska to Puget Sound, Washington. Their oblong shells can grow to over 3 inches wide. The shell is often covered

The wrinkled neck of a truncated mya cannot be fully withdrawn into the shell, creating the look of a compressed accordion.

almost entirely by a flaky, yellowish brown protein layer. This covering extends beyond the shell margins to form a papery tube that encases the fused siphons, or neck.

The common name of this species reflects a squared-off, or truncated, shell margin where the wrinkled neck extends through a wide gap. The oversize neck protrudes from this gap even when the siphons are fully withdrawn. The shell's interior is usually pale yellow or white.

Truncated myas often live in association with little-neck clams and butter clams. These myas are eaten by sea otters, arctic foxes, sunflower stars, king eider ducks, and various fish species.

UGLY CLAMS • Ugly clams take their name from the shell's distorted appearance. They have a thin, gaping shell covered by a thick, brownish protein layer. They prefer to nestle in rock crevices near the low-tide line and below.

Northwest Ugly Clam

ENTODESMA NAVICULA

Northwest ugly clams have a somewhat oblong, fragile shell that measures up to 5½ inches wide.

A rough and misshapen appearance earned the ugly clam its name.

From Western Alaska to Southern California this clam seeks out crevices, holes, and boulder undersides on rocky beaches and attaches itself by threads to dock floats.

The shape of a Northwest ugly clam is determined by its surroundings, the shell conforming to the shape of its chosen home. If it's not living in a tight spot, this clam may be pear-shaped; otherwise, the shape of its home may cause the clam to become significantly deformed.

The rounded hind ends of the shell are gaping and flared, and its interior is glossy white or pearled. The clam's flesh varies in color from a dull orangish brown to brilliant orange.

The shell usually appears wider than it really is because its flaky protein layer extends beyond the shell's true margin. When a shell dries out, this thick outer covering shrinks, causing the thin shell to split and often shatter.

CEPHALOPODS

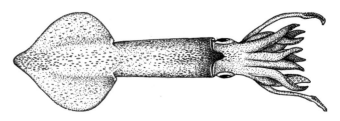

Cephalopods are highly developed molluscs that include squid and octopuses.

Opalescent squid
(Loligo opalescens)

Cephalopods lack the characteristic shell of most molluscs, protecting themselves by other means.

A soft, muscular mantle encases the body and forms a head bearing 2 large complex eyes, a brain, and a mouth equipped with a horny two-part beak (somewhat resembling that of a parrot). The fleshy molluscan foot is modified into a ring of suckered arms extending from the head. The word *cephalopod* is derived from Greek words meaning "head-foot."

Movement is achieved by jet propulsion, water being forced out of the body cavity through a tubular funnel located below the head. Squid and octopuses flee predators by propelling themselves backward, with arms straightened out in the opposite direction of travel.

These creatures defend themselves by biting with their sharp beak or confusing predators with a cloud of ink. This dark fluid is squirted at a predator, creating a smokescreen that blurs its vision and dulls its sense of smell.

Squid live in the open ocean, swimming both forward and backward with the aid of 2 finlike extensions of the body. They have 10 arms surrounding the head and mouth, the longest 2 of which are capable of great extension. These extended arms grab live prey and bring it into the grasp of the other 8 arms. A stiff internal rod serves as a support for the squid's soft body.

OCTOPUSES • Octopuses are sluggish bottom-dwellers with 8 suckered arms of equal length and a saclike body. They can change color rapidly due to large pigmentation cells that can be contracted or expanded by muscles. An octopus usually stalks prey, killing it with its beak and poison saliva.

Some octopuses are giants among invertebrates. The world's largest recorded specimen was a common Pacific octopus caught off western Canada in 1957. It had an arm span of 31½ feet and weighed 600 pounds.

Octopus intelligence has long been a subject of scientific debate. Octopuses have the most complex brain of any living invertebrate, even rivaling that of vertebrates like fish. Octopuses are capable of learning basic tasks, individuals having been taught to find their way through simple mazes or to choose balls of a certain color over and over.

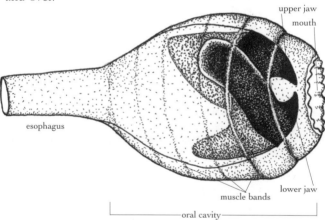

The oral cavity of an octopus (on the body's underside where the 8 tentacles intersect) houses a parrotlike beak made up of upper and lower jaws.

Common Pacific Octopus

OCTOPUS DOFLEINI

Common Pacific octopuses range from Western Alaska to Baja California, inhabiting dens under sizable rocks. The octopus's head and arms vary in color, according

Stranded in a pool at low tide, this octopus turned from whitish gray to reddish orange when the photographer touched it.

to its mood and surroundings, from a mottled white to deep brownish red. Its flesh is folded and wrinkled, and the undersides of its 8 tapered arms bear 2 rows of white suckers each.

In the intertidal zone, common Pacific octopuses may have an arm span of 2 or 3 feet, while the arms of deepwater specimens may span 14 feet or more.

This octopus can capture prey from the protection of its den by reaching out with suckered arms to grasp an unwary animal. Or it may descend on prey while swimming, engulfing it with the arms before disabling it with venom delivered by a bite from the beak. It also crawls across the ocean floor, probing for prey.

These creatures eat a wide variety of invertebrates, fish, and even smaller octopuses. In turn, they are stalked by a host of larger predators, including Alaskans who value them as gourmet seafood or fish bait.

Always handle an octopus gently to avoid receiving a painful bite.

Arthropods are invertebrates with jointed legs, a tough outer skeleton called an exoskeleton that is shed as the animal grows, and an unequally segmented body made up of a head, thorax, and abdomen. The word *arthropoda* means "jointed foot," referring to the jointed appearance of most arthropods' legs. Alaska's marine arthropods include the sea spiders and the crustaceans.

CRUSTACEANS

Crustaceans—including barnacles, isopods, amphipods, shrimps, and crabs—typically have a body divided into head and trunk. The head has 5 pairs of appendages—3 pairs to assist in feeding and 2 pairs of sensory antennae.

The trunk is usually made up of the thorax, with as many as 8 segments, and the abdomen, with up to 6 segments. Most of the segments bear a pair of appendages used for day-to-day functions such as walking, swimming, or feeding. A crustacean's hindmost segment is generally a flattened tailpiece.

Covering a crustacean's body and limbs like a suit of armor is a jointed exoskeleton composed of calcium and a carbohydrate called chitin. When this armor becomes too small for the soft animal within, hormones trigger the crustacean to molt—that is, to shed its exoskeleton. It then secretes a new one.

Crustaceans can regenerate lost limbs through successive molts.

abdominal flap

abdominal flap

The female Dungeness crab (above) has a dome-shaped abdominal flap; the male (left) has a rocket-shaped flap.

BARNACLES • Barnacles are shrimplike animals that live upside down in a chalky domed or columnar shell. Unlike most crustaceans, barnacles remain permanently fixed at one location, forming a protective shell to live in.

Barnacles colonize both shallow and deepwater sites along rocky shorelines. Their volcano-shaped shells may be found adhered to rocks, kelp, shells, driftwood, boat hulls, dock pilings, and plastic marine debris.

A barnacle's head is attached to its shell's base, and 6 pairs of feathery appendages extend from the shell to filter food from the water. These appendages, covered with tiny hairs, rhythmically sweep the ocean for plankton.

A barnacle continually secretes the calcium carbonate shell that surrounds its body, the shell increasing in size as the animal grows. This shell consists of 6 interlocking lateral plates, with 4 additional plates serving as a trapdoor that closes when the barnacle is exposed by a low tide or threatened by a predator.

Inside the shell, barnacles—like other crustaceans—are covered by an exoskeleton that is shed periodically as they grow. During the summer barnacles may molt en masse, their shed exoskeletons forming opaque white mats along riptides or onshore.

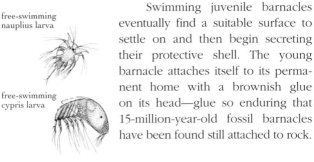

free-swimming
nauplius larva

free-swimming
cypris larva

Swimming juvenile barnacles eventually find a suitable surface to settle on and then begin secreting their protective shell. The young barnacle attaches itself to its permanent home with a brownish glue on its head—glue so enduring that 15-million-year-old fossil barnacles have been found still attached to rock.

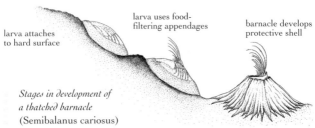

larva attaches
to hard surface

larva uses food-
filtering appendages

barnacle develops
protective shell

Stages in development of a thatched barnacle (Semibalanus cariosus)

Common Gooseneck Barnacle

Common gooseneck barnacles are inhabitants of the open ocean, where they live attached to floating objects such as driftwood,

These barnacles live in the open ocean, attached to floating driftwood and other objects by a rubbery stalk.

plastic, glass bottles, kelp, metal buoys, or cardboard. Massive colonies of this species, attached to logs or other large pieces of debris, occasionally wash up on Alaskan beaches, especially after storms.

The common gooseneck, or goose, barnacle is attached to its home by a fleshy, yellowish brown stalk that is an extension of the animal's head. This rubbery stalk, which cannot be withdrawn into the shell, is capable of bending or twisting movements. The shell is composed of shiny white plates that surround the barnacle's darkly colored body. These barnacles can grow to a length, including the stalk, of over 6 inches.

This barnacle has 6 pairs of reddish brown, feathery appendages that continuously sweep the ocean for food. They catch young fish and various types of plankton.

Gooseneck barnacles take their common name from an old myth that attempted to explain the annual appearance in Britain of juvenile geese. An account published in 1597 told of barnacles growing on trees and, at maturity, opening up to bear geese.

Acorn Barnacle

BALANUS GLANDULA

Acorn barnacles are one of the most abundant seashore creatures on rocky shores from the Aleutian

An acorn barnacle's shell is usually less than ¼ inch wide.

Islands to Southern California. Their small white or gray conical shells adhere to hard surfaces in the intertidal and subtidal zones.

An acorn barnacle's size and shape can vary greatly, depending on conditions—especially the degree of crowding by other barnacles. Uncrowded individuals generally have low shells with prominent furrows and ridges. Crowded barnacles tend to have taller, more columnar shells with fewer ridges.

When exposed by the retreating tide, the shell's hinged top plates close to protect the animal. Walking on a rocky beach, you can sometimes hear these trapdoors closing tighter as your shadow passes over them. Large barnacle beds make a sizzling sound when this occurs.

Acorn barnacles are eaten by dogwinkles, various sea stars, and rough-mantled nudibranchs. Brown bears will smash acorn barnacles and then lick up the mash.

In Alaska, young acorn barnacles may settle on rocks within a broad stretch of beach after a particularly high tide in April, May, or June. This blanket of barnacles resembles a light dusting of snow. Once attached to a hard surface, individuals may survive for 7 to 10 years.

ISOPODS • Marine isopods are buglike crustaceans with a body flattened from top to bottom. They resemble the pill bugs of basements or log undersides. Isopods have 2 compound eyes, 7 pairs of crawling legs, and a number of appendages on the underside that serve as gills or as aids in swimming. Without pinching claws, their only defenses are camouflage and a quick escape. They seek shelter under rocks, on floating docks, or among seaweeds.

Seaweed Isopod

PENTIDOTEA WOSNESENSKII

The seaweed isopod is a stocky invertebrate common to rocky shores from Western Alaska to Southern California. Males tend to be larger than females, growing to about 1½ inches.

A seaweed isopod can change color to match its surroundings soon after molting.

Seaweed isopods are generally dark in color—olive green or dark gray, but also bright green, brown, red, or even mottled pink.

The head has 2 kidney-shaped eyes, a pair of feeding appendages, and 2 long, segmented antennae. The body is made up of 7 large segments, and the rounded tailpiece is tipped with a small, blunt tooth. Pick up one of these animals, and it may use its 14 legs to cling tightly to a finger.

Seaweed isopods eat pieces of algae and, in turn, are eaten by intertidal bottom fish.

AMPHIPODS • Amphipods, commonly called scuds, are active crustaceans with a body that is flattened side to side. They typically have 5 pairs of walking legs, plus 6 pairs of specialized hind appendages for swimming, respiration, and jumping.

Beach Hopper

TRASKORCHESTIA TRASKIANA

Beach hoppers are found near the high-tide line or in the splash zone from Alaska to California, living in washed-up seaweed or burrowing into wet sand while the tide is out.

Though sometimes called sand fleas, beach hoppers do not suck blood from other animals.

Beach hoppers usually have dark gray bodies and legs, though they can also be light gray, green, or salmon pink. The narrow, arched body can be up to ¾ inch long.

During the day, beach hoppers may dig down about an inch into the sand, where they remain until feeding conditions improve with darkness or a higher tide. On the sand, these acrobatic jumpers can leap more than a foot vertically. The body's hind end, by flexing and then straightening sharply out, acts as a springboard.

Beach hoppers eat diatoms and pieces of algae, and are themselves a source of food for nearshore bottom fish, shorebirds, black bears, and land spiders.

CRABS • Crabs are bottom-dwelling crustaceans adapted for a life of crawling. The bodies of crabs (except for hermit crabs) are flattened top to bottom. The carapace—an exoskeleton covering the head and main trunk—is a single wide, flattened shell.

The front of a crab's carapace is equipped with stalked eyes, 2 pairs of antennae, a pair of mouthparts, sensory bristles, and balancing organs. Crabs have 10 legs: generally 4 pairs of walking or swimming legs and 1 forward pair with grasping claws. Crabs generally move sideways, with legs on one side of the body pulling while those on the other side push.

Crabs, like all crustaceans, molt as they grow. A molting crab leaves its old exoskeleton through a split along the rear of the carapace, leaving the shed suit of armor completely intact except for the split. The resulting soft-shelled crab fills itself with water and/or air to stretch its pliable new exoskeleton to a larger size that it can then grow into.

The crab seeks shelter for the time it takes the new exoskeleton to harden—usually at least 48 hours.

Hermit crabs have adapted to life in a borrowed shell. A hermit crab's soft, curved abdomen is anchored into a spiraling snail shell or chalky worm tube by hooklike rear appendages. Some hermit crabs have one enlarged claw that blocks the shell's opening when the crab withdraws into its home. Hermit crabs must acquire new shells as they grow and molt.

egg

pre-zoea larva

zoea larva

Stages in crab development

megalops larva

61

Red King Crab

Red king crabs are Alaska's largest crab species. Found on mud or muddy sand in deep water from Western Alaska to northern British Columbia, these giants can mea-

The rounded carapace of this crab has a forward four-spined projection (the rostrum) and 3 pairs of prominent central spines.

sure almost 5 feet across the outstretched legs and weigh over 20 pounds. A king crab's carapace and 3 pairs of walking legs are dull red in color and covered with sharp spines.

These crabs migrate annually, moving into shallower water in the late winter. After molting and mating, they move back to deeper water. They can travel at speeds of a mile per day and migrate up to 100 miles in a year.

Females produce an average of 240,000 eggs, which are carried under their abdominal flap for almost a year. Juvenile king crabs, after floating in the open ocean for the first 2 months of their life, may be found on rocky shorelines by observant tidepoolers.

Red king crabs eat clams, mussels, snails, sea urchins, sand dollars, sea stars, barnacles, other crabs, tunicates, jellyfish, segmented worms, bryozoans, fish, and algae. These crabs are food for cod, sculpins, yellowfin sole, halibut, and sea otters. Some ribbon worms eat king crab embryos.

This species of king crab, as well as the blue and golden king crabs, are harvested commercially in Alaska.

Orange Hermit Crab

ELASSOCHIRUS GILLI

Orange hermit crabs are brightly colored residents of rocky shores. Living within the low intertidal and shallow subtidal zones, these crabs range from Western Alaska to Puget Sound, Washington.

Large orange hermit crabs wear shells formerly occupied by sizable predatory snails, such as the moon snail shell shown here.

The distinguishing feature is the body's uniformly brilliant orange or orangish red color. They are large for hermit crabs, with the portion of their body protected by the carapace measuring about 1½ inches long on older individuals.

A good way to detect hermit crabs at the water's edge is to look for snail shells that appear to be moving faster than they would with their original occupants inside.

On many Alaskan beaches, nearly every empty shell has been claimed by a hermit crab. To find out if a shell harbors a crab, shake the shell gently, then hold it up to your ear. If it is occupied, the crab inside will make a faint squeaking sound as it readjusts its body.

Orange hermit crabs are opportunistic feeders, with a diet that includes dead animals, fish and snail eggs, tube worms, lamp shells, other hermit crabs, and pieces of algae. Bottom fish and large crabs prey on orange hermit crabs.

Bairði Tanner Crab

CHIONOECETES BAIRDI

Bairdi tanner crabs, living primarily on soft bottoms in deep water, range from Western Alaska to Puget Sound, Washington. The carapace of these large crabs can

Bairði tanner crabs can measure 3 feet from leg tip to leg tip, with males occasionally weighing over 4 pounds.

be more than 7 inches wide, while the width across the entire body with legs outstretched can be 2 or 3 feet.

The crab's carapace and legs are light brown (though more pink in recently molted animals), and the underside is yellowish white. Legs, claws, and the carapace margin have short spines.

A female tanner crab molts for the last time when she is about to produce her first set of eggs, at 5 or 6 years of age. Each year thereafter she may brood as many as 424,000 eggs for about one year under her abdominal flap. The young crabs hatch in spring or early summer, when plankton is most available. Tanner crabs may live as long as 14 years.

Tanner crabs prey on mussels, clams, snails, other crabs, shrimps, and worms, as well as scavenging on dead fish. They provide food for fish and humans. Bairdi and the closely related Opilio tanner crabs are caught in baited pots in Alaska. Tanner crabs are commonly marketed as snow crab.

Horse Crab

TELMESSUS CHEIRAGONUS

Horse (or helmet) crabs are fast-moving crabs of algae-covered shorelines from Western Alaska to Northern California. This species prefers dense seaweed beds, especially eelgrass, on rocks and sand.

The horse crab, common where seaweed is abundant, is easily recognized by its five-sided carapace and its covering of bristles.

Younger horse crabs are usually greenish yellow, changing to yellowish brown as they age. Older crabs exhibit red and orange mottling.

The five-sided carapace, reaching a length of about 4 inches and a width of about 5 inches, has a distinctly jagged margin with 6 large teeth along the crab's sides, behind the eyes. The carapace, long walking legs, and claws are covered with bristles (giving the horse crab the additional name of hairy crab).

While exploring a beach, you may come across what appears to be a dead horse crab. But if the carapace separates easily from the rest of the exoskeleton when you lift it up, and only the gill coverings are found inside, you are simply holding the cast-off remains of a crab that has recently molted. The crab itself is probably alive and well, roaming the ocean floor in a new suit of armor.

Horse crabs scavenge for dead invertebrates and fish, and prey on other crabs. They are eaten by bottom fish and are a favorite food of common Pacific octopuses.

Dungeness Crab

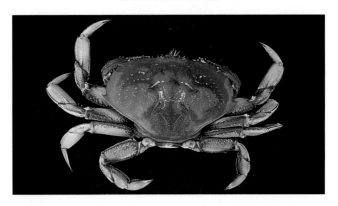

Dungeness crabs, or dungies, are heavy-bodied crabs that live on sand or mud bottoms from Western Alaska to Baja California.

This crab's brownish, D-shaped carapace is nearly twice as wide as it is long and lacks spines.

The crab's spineless, fan-shaped carapace, measuring up to 10 inches wide in large males, may be reddish brown, grayish brown, or brownish purple. The crab's underside and its short walking legs with flattened terminal segments are yellowish; its heavy claws have whitish tips.

Dungeness crabs prefer eelgrass beds or soft substrates in relatively shallow water, most often less than 90 feet. They move into shallower water in the summer to molt and breed, after which females brood as many as 2½ million eggs under their abdominal flap.

A Dungeness crab's diet can include small fish, clams, mussels, abalones, worms, shrimps, other crabs, and dead marine organisms. Larger Dungeness crabs actively prey on juveniles of their own species.

These crabs are eaten by sculpins, herring, salmon, and other crabs. To escape predators, they can quickly burrow backward into the sand or loose mud, leaving only their eyes and mouthparts exposed.

Alaskans take males of this species in baited pots both commercially and for personal use. Crabs that successfully avoid hungry fish or traps may live for 8 to 13 years.

Brachiopods

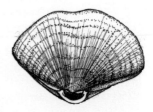

Brachiopods are shelled inverte- *Side view and underside of*
brates that look like clams, but *transverse lamp shell*
they aren't related. One significant difference is that brachiopods remain permanently attached to a hard surface by
a flexible, fleshy stalk. This stalk extends through an opening between a groove in the upper shell's overhanging
edge and a notch in the lower shell's edge, and attaches
the animal to a site in relatively deep, cold waters along
rocky coasts.

Brachiopods are often referred to as lamp or lantern
shells because the larger upper shell in some species, when
turned upside down, resembles a type of oil lamp used by
early Greeks and Romans.

The animal inside of the 2 unequal chalky shells is
completely different from the clams. A feeding apparatus
called the lophophore occupies more than half of the
shells' internal space. This structure is a delicate double
loop bearing hundreds of tiny tentacles. When the shell is
slightly open, hairs on the tentacles beat to draw in food-
laden water. Plankton and drifting organic material are
trapped by the hairs and mucus and brought to the mouth,
which lies in the middle of the loop.

Brachiopods are an ancient group of once-populous
marine invertebrates. An impressive fossil record, dating
back more than 600 million years, contains over 30,000 brachiopod species worldwide. Paleontologists use these fos-
sils to date sedimentary rocks.

Transverse Lamp Shell

TEREBRATALIA TRANSVERSA

Transverse lamp shells are a common brachiopod that lives permanently attached to boulder undersides, in rock crevices, or among kelp holdfasts from the

The lamp shell superficially resembles a clam, but feeds differently and anchors itself by means of a fleshy stalk.

Alaska Peninsula to Baja California. It generally lives alone, rather than in colonies.

The two-part hinged shell, usually fan-shaped, may be reddish, brownish, gray, yellow, or white. The shells can have varying amounts of sculpturing, with some nearly smooth and others bearing clearly visible concentric lines intersected by prominent ribs. The shell is bowed in the middle, creating a bent or wavy effect at its margin.

Transverse lamp shells reach their maximum size, sometimes over 2 inches wide, at 9 to 10 years of age.

Predators include true stars and crabs. Crabs are known to chip away at the edge of a lamp shell until the animal's vulnerable soft parts are exposed.

Bryozoans

Bryozoans are microscopic invertebrates that form encrusting, patterned mats or branching growths. The word *bryozoan* comes from the Greek *bryon,* meaning "moss," and *zoion,* meaning "life" or "animal." Colonies that take the form of low, bushy mats can resemble a carpet of moss.

Approximately 300 bryozoan species have been identified along the Pacific coast from Alaska to Mexico. In Alaska, most bryozoans live in deep water, but beachcombers can easily find intertidal species coating rocks, shells, or kelp at low tides. Properly identifying most bryozoan species is difficult without examining specimens under a microscope. Bryozoans can be mistaken for delicate algae, corals, or hydroids.

Bryozoan colony members, called zooids, are microscopic saclike animals, each with a digestive, reproductive, and simple nervous system. Each zooid secretes a chamber of chalky material or protein in which to live. Some zooids are able to seal the chamber with a hinged lid as protection against drying out or being eaten. A bryozoan colony can consist of a few to thousands, even millions, of zooids.

The lophophore, a fold in the body wall of most zooids, extends beyond their boxlike home to collect food. This fold's hairy tentacles create a current that funnels diatoms, bacteria, and other minute organisms or particles toward the animal's mouth. A bryozoan colony also includes individuals specialized for discouraging predators, keeping the colony free of sediment, or caring for eggs.

Predators include sea spiders, king crabs, flatworms, sea stars, and nudibranchs.

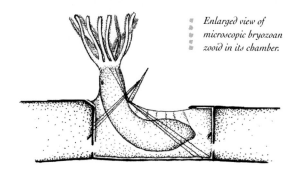

Enlarged view of microscopic bryozoan zooid in its chamber.

Kelp Encrusting Bryozoan

Species of MEMBRANIPORA

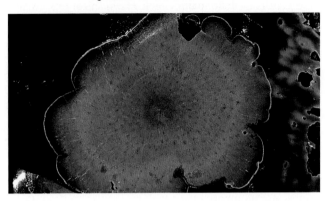

Kelp encrusting bryozoans form lacy, whitish colonies that are most frequently found on flat blades of kelp along the coast

These minute colonial invertebrates often form lacy patterns, visible on this large blade of kelp.

from Alaska to Baja California. They are commonly seen on perennial, sugar, and split kelps within the intertidal zone as well as on kelps attached to harbor floats and pilings.

The colonies are flat and often circular in shape, with the rectangular residence chambers of individuals creating a honeycomb appearance. Young zooids of this species secrete their calcified homes in a series of radiating and branching patterns that resemble a fine lace doily.

This bryozoan's feeding structure and neck region form a trapdoor that seals the chamber after the animal withdraws inside. Retractor muscles running from the base of the feeding structure to the body wall are responsible for pulling an individual hastily into its home when it is disturbed. These muscles shorten at a speed of more than 20 times their length per second, a muscle contraction speed unequaled by any other organism that has been measured.

A close look at a kelp blade encrusted with these bryozoans may turn up one of the nudibranch species that graze on the microscopic animals.

Echinoderms

Echinoderms are fairly large, rough-skinned, or spiny creatures that inhabit a wide range of coastal habitats. Echinoderms—their name derived from Greek words meaning "spiny-skinned"—include the sea stars, brittle stars, sea urchins, sand dollars, and sea cucumbers.

Echinoderms share a number of similar features. The body of an adult echinoderm commonly exhibits 5 equal parts, with a mouth centrally located where the body segments intersect.

Another shared trait is an internal skeleton made up of chalky plates. These plates may be fused to form a continuous skeleton, as in the sea urchins and sand dollars, or they may connect at flexible joints, as in the sea stars. Sea cucumbers contain internal plates that do not connect.

Echinoderms have an internal hydraulic network of canals—the water vascular system—that usually terminates in a series of tube feet. The tube feet, each tipped with a suction cup to aid in movement and capturing food, are important parts of the respiratory system. The animal extends or withdraws its tube feet by modifying its internal water pressure.

Injured echinoderms employ remarkable powers of regenerating body parts.

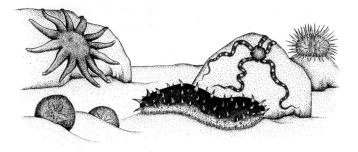

Examples of echinoderms (from upper left): morning sun star; northern sand dollars; California sea cucumber; daisy brittle star; red sea urchin

71

Sea Stars

Sea stars are some of the most eye-catching shoreline creatures in Alaska, ranging in color from deep blues, greens, and purples to brilliant oranges, reds, and yellows, as well as subdued tones of brown and gray. They bear no relationship to fish, as their commonly used nickname, starfish, might suggest.

The sea stars found in Alaska have from 5 to 24 arms, or rays, the undersides of which sport rows of hollow tube feet tipped with small suckers. Most sea stars pump water through a pale-colored sieve plate (the madreporite) on their top side. Water enters the body cavity and eventually reaches the tube feet, which can then cling to a surface and pull the animal along.

A sea star's skeleton is made up of many limy plates embedded in the skin, while bumps and spines give the skin an uneven texture. If an Alaskan sea star loses any body part (other than the central disk), it slowly regrows it. Larger species of sea stars may live as long as 40 years.

Sea stars do not allow organisms to take up residence on their backs. Tiny pincers nip off any hitchhikers. To see how efficient these pincers are, gently place one of the stockier sea stars—a true star, for example—upside down on your forearm. Leave it there for a few seconds, and the pincers will attach to the hairs of your arm. Removing the star will be like separating pieces of Velcro.

The hunched-up posture of a sea star indicates that it is feeding.

Leather Star

DERMASTERIAS IMBRICATA

Leather stars inhabit low intertidal and subtidal rocks from South-central Alaska to Baja California, growing to diameters (arm tip to arm tip) of more than 10 inches.

Leather stars appear rather slimy when wet because the animal's spines don't extend above the leathery skin.

These stout sea stars have 5 wide, webbed rays (or arms) and a thick, broad central disk.

This star's spineless inflated upper surface is red, brownish red, or orangish red, mottled with gray or blue. A yellowish spot is the sieve plate that takes in and expels seawater.

On each ray's pale yellow or cream-colored underside are 4 rows of suckered tube feet that lie within a deep furrow bordered by flesh-covered, knobby spines.

This species is also called the garlic star because of its sulfurous odor. Usually the star must be held directly under your nose to really smell the pungent aroma.

Yellow scale worms are attracted to the scent of a leather star. These 3- to 4-inch-long hitchhikers, which do the sea star no harm, have been documented on the undersides of at least 9 sea star species in the North Pacific, including leather stars.

A leather star's diet may include sea anemones, hydroids, sea cucumbers, encrusting sponges, sea pens, sea urchins, bryozoans, and other sea stars.

Sun Star

SOLASTER STIMPSONI

Sun stars are colorful residents of rocky, sandy, or muddy shores from Western Alaska to Northern California. Capable of growing to

A sun star's skin has a texture much like that of rough sandpaper due to clusters of tiny spines.

more than 16 inches in diameter, these soft-bodied sea stars have 10 to 12 slim, tapering rays and a slightly raised central disk.

The large disk can be nearly a quarter of the sun star's diameter and on its upper surface bears a central patch of blue-gray or purple. A streak of this same purplish color radiates from the central patch down the length of each ray, creating a sunburst design on the sea star.

The background color on the sun star's top side is typically yellowish orange, orange, or reddish orange. On the animal's underside, the tube feet are enveloped in a deep furrow bordered on both edges by the same purplish color displayed on the star's upper surface.

Included in a sun star's diet are sea cucumbers, lamp shells, sea pens, sea squirts, anemones, and worms. In turn, sun stars are preyed upon by foraging gulls at low tide and by a related sea star, the morning sun star *(Solaster dawsoni)*. A sun star under attack by this related species may curl all of its rays upward to form a bowl of arms that the predator can have difficulty maneuvering around.

Blood Star

Brilliant red blood stars add a striking splash of color to tide-pools and low intertidal rocks from the Aleutian Islands to Baja California. These graceful-looking

Groups of short spinelets arranged in an intricate network decorate this bright red star's upper surface.

stars—red, purplish red, orangish, or brownish red—have 5 long, slender rays.

The blood star's central disk is relatively small in relation to the animal's overall size, which can reach 8 inches in diameter.

The undersides of the rays bear deep furrows that enclose the tube feet. A species of yellow scale worm, taking advantage of food scraps left behind by the star, is often found living within one of these grooves.

Blood stars frequently eat sponges and bryozoans by applying their stomach to the encrusting colonies. Or they extend their rays into a food-laden current so that plankton can adhere to mucus on the body's surface and then be transported by minute hairs along tracts to the mouth.

True Star

EVASTERIAS TROSCHELII

True stars are one of the most familiar stars of Alaska's beaches. They inhabit a variety of sites from Western Alaska to Central Califor-

True stars, displaying a wide range of colors, are often numerous in areas where their food is plentiful.

nia, generally preferring shorelines subject to low wave energy. True stars in the intertidal zone grow to about a foot in diameter, while individuals at deeper sites may reach almost twice this size.

The upper surface of these 5-rayed stars may be green, gray, brown, reddish brown, brownish orange, deep purple, or midnight blue, and may be variably patterned with prominent white spines and less visible pincers.

This star's long, tapering rays extend from a relatively small central disk. The animal's spiny underside is yellowish and may house a species of scale worm that closely matches the color of its host.

True stars prey heavily on clams and mussels and also eat barnacles, snails, chitons, and tunicates. Gulls, sea otters, and crabs prey on these stars. Odd-looking true stars—missing from 1 to all 5 arms, and in the process of regenerating them—are often seen on beaches at low tide.

True stars can be confused with ochre stars (*Pisaster ochraceus*). True stars have longer, more slender rays, a smaller central disk, and a less pronounced network of spines on their back.

Little Six-rayed Star

Species of LEPTASTERIAS

Beachcombers in Alaska will find little six-rayed stars clinging tenaciously to the undersides of many rocks. These camouflaged sea stars are abundant residents of boulder

Little six-rayed stars, only a couple of inches in diameter, often match the color of rocks in their environment.

beaches and eelgrass beds from the Alaska Peninsula to Southern California.

Little six-rayed stars measure only 1 or 2 inches in diameter, occasionally growing to over 3 inches. Their upper surface is drab, exhibiting one solid color or a mottling of several shades and often matching the coloration of the surrounding rocks. Olive green, dark gray, brown, yellowish brown, and pink are common colors.

Six broad arms radiate from the central disk, all of which are covered by numerous flattened spines. This sea star's underside is yellowish and sometimes houses a harmless species of scale worm.

Included in this star's diet are acorn barnacles, lined and black leather chitons, and various snails. Bottom fish such as flounders and halibut eat little six-rayed stars.

Take care in trying to remove a six-rayed star from a rock for examination, because it may be caring for its eggs or offspring. In spring and early summer, a female star may brood as many as 500 eggs, which hatch and develop under her central disk.

Sunflower Star

PYCNOPODIA HELIANTHOIDES

Sunflower stars, Alaska's largest sea stars, can be the size of a car tire. They range from the Aleutian Islands to Baja California, living on various surfaces near the low-tide line and farther out.

Having a remarkable ability to regenerate lost limbs, the orange sunflower star shown here is growing 6 new rays.

Sunflower stars have soft, fleshy bodies with broad central disks and up to 24 rays. The color of the upper surface is highly variable: neon orange, blue-green, dark blue, light pink, brown, and dark gray are common shades.

White spines are sometimes visible on the top of the star. Its underside is bright yellow-orange and bears more than 15,000 tube feet that resemble macaroni and cheese.

Sunflower stars are very active, their suckered tube feet pulling them along at 18 inches per minute. Their internal plates are not joined, giving them flexibility but making them susceptible to damage by handling. Extreme care is called for in picking up large, water-filled sunflower stars.

Preferred foods are urchins, usually swallowed whole, and clams, excavated by moving sand or gravel with arms and tube feet and then forced open by pressure from the tube feet. They can also squeeze through tiny openings in crab and shrimp traps, devouring the animals inside.

Morning sun stars, king crabs, bottom fish, and scavenging gulls eat sunflower stars.

BRITTLE STARS

Brittle stars, closely akin to sea stars, differ from their larger relatives in their small, roundish central disk being clearly distinct from the 5 thin rays extending from it. Their sieve plate, through which water enters the animal, is located on the disk's underside rather than on its upper surface as in sea stars. Their tube feet are used for feeding on small organic particles, but not for locomotion. Brittle stars are named for their ability to shed rays when harassed; these limbs are soon regenerated.

Daisy Brittle Star

OPHIOPHOLIS ACULEATA

Daisy brittle stars live on rock undersides and in kelp holdfasts from arctic Alaska to Central California. They are light-sensitive, taking refuge beneath rocks or algae when exposed by an outgoing tide.

Each looking like a piece of modern art, these stars use a snakelike motion of their rays to shuffle over pebbles.

This star's 5 long, tapering rays can extend up to 5½ inches from tip to tip, and the scalloped central disk has a lobe between each ray. Tiny blunt spines along each ray give these stars a prickly look.

The disk's upper surface may exhibit one solid color or have a mottled design of maroon, brownish red, yellowish brown, or orange. These animals scavenge small crustaceans, worms, and organic particles in areas exposed to strong currents.

SEA URCHINS

Sea urchins, sometimes called sea eggs or porcupines of the sea, are echinoderms with a pincushion-like body. Spines cover the body, protecting the fragile skeleton as well as providing a stiltlike movement for the animal across the ocean floor.

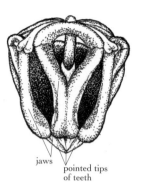

jaws — pointed tips of teeth

Chewing mouthparts (collectively called Aristotle's lantern) of an urchin

Delicate tube feet, capable of great extension, emerge through tiny pores in the skeleton. These are used in locomotion, securing food, respiration, and sensory functions.

An urchin's pincers remove debris, aid in capturing food, or ward off predators by means of toxins. The animal's sieve plate, for taking in and expelling water, is centrally located on its upper surface.

In the middle of an urchin's underside is its mouth, surrounded by 5 teeth. The tips of these long, tapering teeth converge to form a remarkable chewing structure known as Aristotle's lantern. Resembling an ancient Greek lantern in appearance, this apparatus is used for grazing on algae as well as for chopping food that is brought to the mouth into digestible pieces.

Despite their spiny armor, urchins become food for sea stars, crabs, fish, otters, gulls, and humans. Urchins can regenerate damaged spines, tube feet, and pincers.

Sand dollars, highly prized but rarely found by beach-combers in Alaska, are flattened sea urchins with much reduced spines, tube feet, and pincers. Waves of coordinated spine movements allow them to burrow through the sand in which they live.

Green Sea Urchin

STRONGYLOCENTROTUS DROEBACHIENSIS

From arctic Alaska to Puget Sound, Washington, green sea urchins are one of the coast's most abundant sizable invertebrates. These spiny animals prefer pro-tected sites on sandy or rocky shores from the midintertidal zone to water half a mile deep.

Each spine on an urchin is a single calcium carbonate crystal that grows throughout the animal's life.

This urchin's overall coloration is commonly light green, sometimes highlighted by reddish tones, but may also be whitish green and purplish white.

Green sea urchins are generally less than 2 inches wide and are thought to have a life span of 4 to 8 years. They are characteristically covered with fairly short, crowded spines. Suckered tube feet, looking much like purple hairs, extend well beyond the tips of the spines.

These light-sensitive urchins prefer to live under rocks or algae. Where boulders or substantial algae are absent, they will wear bits of algae, pebbles, or shells on their upper surface, securing these in place with their tube feet.

In addition to grazing on algae and diatoms, this species will eat injured urchins, stranded jellyfish, bryo-zoans, tube worms, and dead fish. These urchins are preyed on by sea stars, sea anemones, hairy tritons, king crabs, otters, foxes, fish, and birds. Alaskan divers harvest the urchins for edible eggs, or roe, in the body cavity.

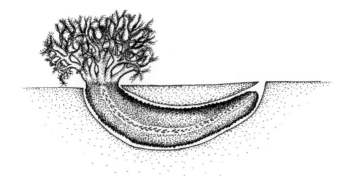

Sea cucumbers are soft-bodied echinoderms with the small chalky plates of the skeleton deeply embedded and scattered through-out the skin. External spines and pincers are absent.

A red sea cucumber, with its mop of feeding tentacles reaching into the water above its burrow.

Narrow rows of tube feet, though not always visible, extend lengthwise down a sea cucumber's elongated, wormlike body. At one end of the body, a mass of sticky, branching tentacles called the mop surrounds the mouth, trapping tiny marine plants and animals. The mop is peri-odically withdrawn into the mouth, where the food is stripped off and then transported to the gut for digestion.

Sea cucumbers may lie on top of sand, mud, and gravel, or seek the protection of boulder undersides. Three to 5 bands of tube feet aid in movement. Sea cucumbers may burrow so that only the mop is exposed for feeding; the mops look like lacy flowers when seen underwater. These animals can also eat their way into the ocean floor, digesting organic material as they burrow.

Sea cucumbers, even though many have foul-tasting skin, are preyed on by a host of invertebrates and fish. If stressed, a sea cucumber has the ability to rid its body of its internal organs through the anus located opposite the mouth. This seemingly self-destructive act provides a pur-suer with a small meal; meanwhile, the cucumber escapes to regenerate its lost organs.

Red Sea Cucumber

CUCUMARIA MINIATA

Red sea cucumbers, ranging from the Aleutian Islands to Central California, seek out rock crevices *Tube feet are situated in double longitudinal rows on red sea cucumbers.* and undersides within the low intertidal and subtidal zones.

Resembling their namesake garden vegetable in shape, these animals are usually brick-red—though pinkish, purplish, or bright orange individuals can also be found. Their cylindrical body, covered by elastic skin that feels like soft leather, bears 5 double rows of tube feet.

Interlaced bands of strong muscle make up for the animal's lack of a rigid skeleton. These muscles contract and expand to change the sea cucumber's shape and length. When fully stretched, red sea cucumbers can be over 9 inches long.

This animal crawls over the ocean floor by stretching and contracting and pulling itself along with short tube feet. When burrowing, the feeding tentacles, or mop, clear away debris from the animal's forward end. This end then swells, and longitudinal muscles contract to pull the body into the newly enlarged space.

Buried red sea cucumbers extend their mop into passing currents to trap food. A disturbed sea cucumber rapidly pulls the mop into its mouth, retreating fully into the burrow. Individuals surviving predation by sun stars, crabs, fish, and scavenging gulls may live 5 years or more.

Tunicates

Tunicate larva

Tunicates are saclike invertebrates, most of which remain anchored to a hard surface or fixed object for their entire life. Included in this fascinating group are sea peaches (a solitary tunicate) and sea pork (a tunicate that lives in colonies).

Tunicates derive their name from their leathery body walls—or tunics. A pair of openings, the siphons, are located opposite a tunicate's point of attachment, helping to distinguish these animals from other attached bottom-dwelling organisms.

Their nickname, sea squirts, comes from their habit of releasing a jet of water from one or both siphons when touched.

Tunicates are more closely related to vertebrates than are any other group of spineless marine creatures in Alaska. The drifting larvae of tunicates, resembling tadpoles, possess a primitive form of backbone called a notochord, a nerve cord along the back, and gill slits in the throat region.

A tunicate larva cannot feed itself. With food reserves lasting perhaps only several hours, the planktonic larva quickly settles to the ocean floor. As the saclike body with siphons develops, the notochord and tail disappear.

Sea Peach

Sea peaches are solitary bottom-dwelling sea squirts that range from arctic Alaska to Puget Sound, Washington. They look like an inflated leathery sack (and remotely like a stretched peach) when feeding.

This sea peach, its siphons fully extended, is filtering microscopic plankton from the surrounding water.

The sea peach's slender, upright body is red, orange, or yellowish. The body, granular and even in appearance, sports a pair of 4-lobed siphons that look like small crosses when withdrawn.

These living sacks of water filter tiny plants and animals from the ocean by means of an internal food-trapping structure, which also serves as a site for the animal's respiration. Water is brought into the body cavity through one siphon, and plankton is filtered out by the feeding structure's mucous web. Food is then transported to the animal's esophagus and stomach.

Young sea peaches generally settle on sheltered rocks in the low intertidal and subtidal zones where currents provide plenty of plankton. Anchored and supplied with a fairly constant source of food, a sea peach can grow to almost 6 inches in height.

Along Alaska's coast sea peaches are preyed on by frilled dogwinkles, hairy tritons, nudibranchs, sharks, skates, and other bottom fish.

Alaska's rocky coastal areas provide endless opportunities for you to become personally acquainted with the seashore creatures featured in this guidebook. When the tide recedes, marine invertebrates seek shelter where they can remain moist. This often means the isolated pockets of standing water that are known as tidepools. It also means the underside of rocks, the interior of tiny caves or empty seashells, and beneath mats of marine algae.

Discovering these invertebrate retreats is one of the thrills of tidepooling—which is simply the exploration of the shore when the tide is low. You may go tidepooling in one of Alaska's many coastal stretches that present a jumble of gravel and boulders, without any actual tidepools. No matter. It's tidepooling just the same.

WHERE TO GO • With thousands of miles of coastline to choose from, how does a tidepooler in Alaska know where to go? In a sense, anywhere will do. It's all seashore. But some shores are easier to get to than others. Some have a better selection of animal habitats than others. Some are just plain more fun than others.

Here are a few of our favorites:

Kachemak Bay, on the Kenai Peninsula, has an abundance of great tidepooling beaches. Bishop's Beach, accessible from a parking lot at the end of Beluga Street in Homer, is worth exploring on virtually any low tide. Easy walking across the exposed sand to boulder patches at the water's edge brings you to a cornucopia of marine life.

On Kachemak Bay's south side, practically any accessible beach is worth visiting. The Center for Alaskan Coastal Studies, a nonprofit organization with a marine field station in Peterson Bay, adjoining Kachemak Bay, offers daily guided excursions throughout the summer to one of the finest tidepooling spots in the state. The center's naturalists share a wealth of knowledge and enthusiasm for Alaska's marine invertebrates. Call the center at (907)235-6667 for information.

In Seward, beachgoers can reach the intertidal zone from the end of Lowell Point Road. Follow this gravel road to its end and head south along the shore toward exposed

rocks to find the splashes of color that indicate a rich marine ecosystem. Be careful to return to your starting point before the tide gets *When the tide goes out along Alaska's coast, a fascinating world of marine creatures is unveiled.*
too high, as the shores of Resurrection Bay are steep cliffs.

Kodiak Island is rich in marine fauna as well. Alaska State Parks offers free guided tidepooling excursions. Fort Abercrombie State Park's rangers lead walks for visitors of all ages during morning minus tides in the summer. Outings usually last for two hours and rubber boots are recommended. Visit the park's visitor center north of the city of Kodiak or call (907)486-6339 for dates and times.

In Southeast Alaska, beaches around Sitka will provide hours of excitement for tidepoolers. Some of the area's best spots include Halibut Point, John Brown's Beach, Samson Cove, Three Entrance Bay, and the beach bordering Totem National Park. Contact the Sitka state parks district office at (907)747-6249 for information on guided beach walks during the summer. The Sitka boat harbor is also a fun place to poke around for invertebrates. Lie on your belly and watch sea life beneath the dock.

FINDING YOUR OWN SPECIAL SPOT •

The places discussed above are just a fraction of the tide-pooling treasures of Alaska. You can find your own spot by knowing what to look for in a tidepooling location.

The greatest diversity of creatures, and therefore the

best tidepooling, is found at the edge of clear water along rocky shores and in places with extreme tidal fluctuations. Go where the water is not muddied by soil runoff or glacial silt. Look for algae-covered boulders and gravel on rocky shorelines.

You'll have the best luck spotting marine animals as they feed, fight, or rest if you do your viewing from the edge of a tidepool rather than being in it. For the best viewing on stretches of beach with no actual tidepools, avoid walking in the water.

Boat harbors and floating docks are also excellent places to look for marine invertebrates. Here you can investigate the constantly submerged marine life attached to a dock's underside or the animals living on a section of wood piling exposed by the dropping tide. Be sure to examine growths of algae under a dock for invertebrates that might live among and on these seaweeds.

The best—that is, the lowest—tides for daytime tidepooling occur for about 2 weeks out of each month from late March through September during the full and new moons. Give yourself enough time to explore the shoreline before the tide turns and water rushes back onto the beach. Plan to arrive at the shore at least an hour before the tide reaches its lowest point. And keep track of the tide once you're there so you don't become stranded on a bar or a rock outcropping or beneath a cliff.

You can also tidepool at night. Evening excursions allow you to explore the coast during winter's lowest tides. Just remember to bring a flashlight or lantern.

Marine animals have adapted to withstand all sorts of conditions, so they will probably fare well during stormy or windy weather. But these conditions will affect your comfort. No matter what the season, dress warmly, and wear rubber boots with thick soles and good tread for walking on slippery rocks. It's a good idea to dress in layers for the cool and changeable Alaskan seashore weather. A pair of neoprene gloves is invaluable for keeping hands warm when handling cold, wet rocks and animals.

PHOTO TIPS • You need patience to photograph marine invertebrates. Finding a photogenic creature and then waiting for proper light and the desired position of the animal can take lots of time.

Many creatures live in sheltered, dark spaces, so you may need a fast-speed film (200 or 400 ASA) to compensate for limited light. Using a flash on overcast days can bring out definition and color; however, when used on wet animals and surfaces, a flash can make your subject appear too shiny. Fast-speed film will also help stop an animal's movement in your photo.

For shooting up close, a macro lens works best. If you're photographing a tidepool scene and want creatures under the water to show up well, add a polarizer to the lens to eliminate any sheen of light on the water's surface.

Bring along a towel for drying your hands between the wet business of setting up your subject and touching your camera. Or ask a friend to do the messy work for you.

The material in the following section, on safeguarding the health and habitat of the marine creatures you find, is also important information for photographers.

How to Be a Friend to Alaska's Marine Invertebrates • The shoreline
is home to an incredible number and variety of marine creatures, and each time we walk across the intertidal zone of a beach, we run the risk of disrupting their lives. Fragile marine communities can be irreversibly damaged by trampling even when we mean no harm. We're kinder to these animals when we walk instead of run, and when we place our feet where they will do the least damage.

Tidepoolers often move rocks to get a look at the organisms that find shelter underneath. It takes care to move a rock without injuring the animals—and to put the rock back in its original spot after your inspection in such a way that the creatures aren't hurt or left exposed to predators or to the drying effects of wind and sun.

Responsible tidepoolers don't remove animals from the shore. If you decide to briefly study an animal, you can simply return it to its home when you're through. Clam diggers who uncover creatures other than their quarry can return rocks to where they found them and fill holes back in with the mud they removed.

LOOKING FOR SOUVENIRS? • If you want to collect souvenirs of a trip to the beach—shells or driftwood or such—take care to not collect live animals. Invertebrates stranded by the outgoing tide may look dead even though they are very much alive and awaiting the water's return. Sea stars left high and dry lose water from within their body cavities and look quite emaciated, but they're in fine health.

If you mistakenly take one of these animals home, the unfortunate dying and then rotting creature will produce a pungent odor not soon to be forgotten. A hermit crab removed from the beach will reward you with the same result; they can't survive in terrariums the way that land hermit crabs can.

Even seemingly empty snail shells aren't good candidates for collection because invertebrates recycle them as housing. The "empty" shell will most likely harbor a resident crab.

IF YOU'RE AN AQUARIUM COLLECTOR • Animals removed from the beach and placed for an extended period of time in sealed plastic bags or buckets without aerators have little chance of surviving. Intertidal invertebrates have specific life requirements that are very difficult to provide, even in a closed saltwater aquarium. Unless you have a well-thought-out plan for quickly transferring seashore animals to an established cold-water marine aquarium, invertebrates are better off left in their environment.

If you do have the means for keeping marine creatures alive and healthy, remove only minimal numbers of any given species. The spot you are collecting in may be one of only a handful of suitable micro-habitats available to that species. It might be abundant where you are, but otherwise uncommon in Alaska. The state Department of Fish and Game has information on the permits required for collecting marine invertebrates.

Suggested Reading

Abbott, R. Tucker. *A Guide to Field Identification: Seashells of North America*. New York: Golden Press, 1986.

Barr, Lou, and Nancy Barr. *Under Alaskan Seas*. Anchorage: Alaska Northwest Publishing Company, 1983.

Behrens, David W. *Pacific Coast Nudibranchs*. Monterey, Calif.: Sea Challengers, 1991.

Carefoot, Thomas H. *Pacific Seashores: A Guide to Intertidal Ecology*. Seattle: University of Washington Press, 1977.

Coulombe, Deborah A. *The Seaside Naturalist: A Guide to Study at the Seashore*. New York: Simon & Schuster, 1992.

Foster, Nora R. *Intertidal Bivalves: A Guide to the Common Marine Bivalves of Alaska*. Fairbanks: University of Alaska Press, 1991.

Gotshall, Daniel W. *Guide to Marine Invertebrates: Alaska to Baja California*. Monterey, Calif.: Sea Challengers, 1994.

Jensen, Gregory C. *Pacific Coast Crabs and Shrimps*. Monterey, Calif.: Sea Challengers, 1995.

Kozloff, Eugene N. *Invertebrates*. Philadelphia: Saunders College Publishing, 1990.

————. *Seashore Life of the Northern Pacific Coast*. Seattle: University of Washington Press, 1983.

McConnaughey, Bayard H., and Evelyn McConnaughey. *Pacific Coast: The Audubon Society Nature Guides*. New York: Alfred A. Knopf, 1985.

Meinkoth, Norman A. *The Audubon Society Field Guide to North American Seashore Creatures*. New York: Alfred A. Knopf, 1997.

Morris, Percy A. *A Field Guide to Pacific Coast Shells: The Peterson Field Guide Series*. Boston: Houghton Mifflin Company, 1980.

Niesen, Thomas M. *Beachcomber's Guide to Marine Life of the Pacific Northwest*. Houston: Gulf Publishing Company, 1997.

Paine, Stefani Hewlett. *Beachwalker: Sea Life of the West Coast*. Vancouver, British Columbia: Douglas & McIntyre, 1992.

Ricketts, Edward F., Jack Calvin, and Joel W. Hedgpeth. Revised by D. W. Phillips. *Between Pacific Tides*. 5th ed. Stanford, Calif.: Stanford University Press, 1985.

Wrobel, David, and Claudia Mills. *Pacific Coast Pelagic Invertebrates: A Guide to the Common Gelatinous Animals*. Monterey, Calif.: Sea Challengers and Monterey Bay Aquarium, 1998.

Index

Alaska Northwest Books™ is proud to publish another book in its Alaska Pocket Guide series, designed with the curious traveler in mind. Ask for more books in this series at your favorite bookstore, or contact Alaska Northwest Books™.

ALASKA NORTHWEST BOOKS™
An imprint of Graphic Arts Center Publishing Company
P.O. Box 10306, Portland, OR 97296-0306 / 503-226-2402